AF265006

Poured
me a
glass
of
Life

"Move over clouds, give me the sky,
I have me my wings
And I'm ready to fly"

# Poured me a glass of Life

One Woman's journey of choosing Life over the bottle

## Denise Cloughley
with
Dr. Gavin A. Jones

TITLE: Poured Me a Glass of Life

By: Denise Cloughley with Dr Gavin A. Jones
Editor: Angee Costa

Editor: For Dr Jones, Rainy Wharf
Cover Design and book interior: Giovanni Misagrande
Illustrator: Giovanni Misagrande

First printed and published in Aotearoa, New Zealand in 2020

Printed by: BookPrinting.co.nz, at Auckland, New Zealand

ISBN-Paperback   978-0-473-54956-5
ISBN- E-book      978-0-473-54957-2

A catalogue record of this book is available from Te Puna Matauranga o Aotearoa National Library of New Zealand.

**For my Mum and my Dad**
Thank you, for always being here for me,
as I promise I'll always be here for you.
I love you both so much.

# CONTENTS


Foreword..................................................................................9

Chapter 1:   I'm Possible ........................................................13

Chapter 2:   Nasty Realities....................................................17

Chapter 3:   Life before my dance with Sav............................19

Chapter 4:   Queenstown........................................................23

Chapter 5:   First Loves ..........................................................26

Chapter 6:   Digging Holes .....................................................28

Chapter 7:   Friendship like rust, it never sleeps-....................30

Chapter 8:    Building a Career ...............................................36

Chapter 9:   Children of the Heart..........................................43

Chapter 10: Panic! ..................................................................47

Chapter 11: Relapse................................................................63

Chapter 12: The last train stop. ..............................................67

Chapter 13: It's all over rova at Nova......................................71

Chapter 14: Next stop, basement ............................................80

Chapter 15: The great escape ..................................................83

Chapter 16: On the Run..........................................................86

Chapter 17: Bella Domani .......................................................98

Chapter 18: First, I fight for freedom ...................................102

Chapter 19: The Final Days...................................................105

Chapter 20: Purgatory ..........................................................108

Chapter 21: The beginning of the end...................................117

Chapter 22: The day I met HOPE.................................................130

Chapter 23: Mental health matters .............................................134

Chapter 24: Shutting Down .......................................................137

Chapter 25: Bright Lights and Dark Places .................................140

Chapter 26: HALTS ...................................................................149

Chapter 27: New, new beginnings .............................................154

Chapter 28: Seeking Solace .......................................................160

Chapter 29: Seeking Solace is born ...........................................166

Chapter 30: Intervention (or Interruption) ...............................171

Chapter 31: Sam .......................................................................176

Chapter 32: Lizzie ....................................................................185

Chapter 33: Families Matter ......................................................189

Chapter 34: Mark and Kim .......................................................192

Chapter 35: Happily Stranded in 2020 ......................................197

Post Chapter: From a clinical psychologist's view......................205

Acknowledgments .....................................................................225

# FOREWORD

I opened my laptop and accidentally wrote a book. From my heart and mind, I allowed my thoughts, emotions, and memories to pour out unimpeded. As the memories surfaced, I let the words flow. Many of those memories are pleasant and life-giving. Others are horrifying. Most have been buried, though I have marked their final resting places in case I have to dig them up. I have revisited my years, past and present; the years that comprise my lifetime. It is a rich tapestry of moments of true love and deep despair, blinding beauty, gnarled shame, crushing regret, and unfathomable happiness. What is life if not a muddied mixture of all things? Some days are beautiful, and some are not. But the lovely can never be known without the ugly. Strength is perfected in times of weakness. Joy is enhanced by the knowledge of sorrow. We live and we learn. We fall, we rise, we err, and then we learn some more.

I've done some crazy things in my life and experienced a big gulp of adversity, whether through no fault of my own or not, with the people, places, and things I have encountered. I have said my forever sorrys for the pain I've caused others and myself. But rather than focus on my mistakes, I embrace the pride and joy that comes from the courage I found to change, put my life in order, and amend my ways.

True, the failures hurt. After all, no one asked too much of me. All they really wanted was my love. They wanted me to be present and intentional in my relationships with them. They wanted the wife in me, the mother in me, the daughter, the sister, and the friend. They did not demand perfection—just perseverance. Most of all, they wanted me to live well and live long, to say, 'No more' to everything that distracted me from their love and sought to destroy me. They wanted me to dare to believe I could do it.

As I write these words, a pandemic grips my adopted country and the entire world. Yet here I sit in the moment amongst the peace and beauty and never-ending smiles of Thailand. There is work to be done, and people to see, but I am not filled with anxiety or fear. I patiently wait for the borders to open again, to let me go over the oceans, to hold my grandbaby boy who is both my blood and my heart. As I wait and long to be with him, my love for him grows. I ponder how I can miss someone so greatly whom I have never met. But that is the power of love—true love. It is not bound by time or space. It does not require history. It fuses two hearts almost involuntarily, holding them forever locked despite being apart.

Sometimes you just don't know if something is missing until you find it; you feel it in your heart, in your mind, and in your soul. You feel it in the bones of you. That is what powers your faith that all things are possible. You believe you can, and then you just go in search of your destiny. I did, and with that, I finally met **'me'**.

"The greatest glory in living lies not in never falling, but in rising every time we fall" – *Nelson Mandela*

CHAPTER 1

# *I'm Possible*

I met Kat at a rehabilitation center in Thailand in August 2019. At the time, I was working with four clients. As soon as I laid eyes on her, I was overcome with sorrow. A fragmented human being, the sadness behind her eyes pierced my heart. I had seen that look before, too many times before. If this girl could not find worth in herself, she would never make it. It wasn't just her alcohol-soaked skin, sunken eyes, bloated stomach, and telltale yellowing indicating damaged organs that caught my attention. It was in her eyes, a look of brokenness, resignation to sad empty brokenness.

Kat died today in a hospice in Australia surrounded by her forever loving family. She couldn't beat the bottle, so the bottle beat her. She was 39 years old. People said all the words one says at such times like, "We hope she is at peace now," and "finally she's at rest". *I hope <u>they</u> find peace*, I screamed in the silence of my heart. That they now had peace from the beast of addiction and its ugly claws that scratched away at their picture of a beautiful family. Kat's just dead.

I really liked Kat; she was a special, caring, kind spirit. In another life, she had served as an ER nurse who was highly regarded in her workplace as I later learned. But in the months following her discharge from rehab to a little condo nearby where I lived in Chiang Mai, Thailand, I chose not to get any closer to her. I'd spun the "You're one drink away," amongst many other lines, but I just knew in my bones that her chances of stopping were slim, and nothing I said or did would change that. Her death spiral was strong, and she had lost the will to fight against the tide. I never give up on anyone until I'm standing over their grave, but she'd given up on herself, and the only one that could have saved Kat was Kat.

She wasn't my client but that didn't matter. I had learned a long, long time ago that people have to want recovery for themselves. They have to want it more than their next breath because it would take every ounce of their strength and determination to seize it. For whatever reason, the choice to change yourself is deeply internal. The best thing to do was stand back, wait, and watch. It's a helpless place to be, knowing there wasn't a damn thing I could do.

I've seen it from both sides now and know that there are only two types of people; the ones who fight and the ones who die. I don't judge. There but for the grace of God, go I, I would be dead too. I *was* dying. I *was* Kat until I made a choice not to be.

I've met many Kats in my years of researching rehab centers from the inside out. As I like to refer to it, I was getting my PhD. in alcoholism. I don't know the numbers; I remember the ones who fought their way out of the forest. And I remember the names of those who didn't make it. I'm glad I'm not a numbers girl. I don't want to count, because it diminishes the individual and makes them a little more than a statistic. I want to cry for each of them when the battle is over, but I rarely cry. Instead, I get angry, and then I get even.

I show people how not to die. I guide them to good people and places who will show them how to live. And for the ones who want to live, it often works. For every Kat, Linda, and Wayne in my life who didn't make it, there is Sam, Lizzie, and Susan that did. And when I see them living, fighting, and believing, I raise my finger to addiction. I whisper, *Screw you, Addiction. I'll show you who the boss is.*

The reason I finally decided to put my world into words is to scream out a message; A good, peaceful, and calm life is possible. Take a close look at the word **Impossible** and separate the syllables. There you have it; **I'm possible.**

I want every person I meet to shout, 'I'm possible'. The **me** I want to be is possible. It is possible to live the life you were destined to have free of addiction, and it's not as hard as it sounds. You just must have one solid mantra as a foundation; **I believe I can, so I will. I'm possible.** Look deeply inside yourself, at what makes you 'you,' then get a really good clinical psychologist to help free you of weights you no longer need to carry or own. They represent the emotional and psychological baggage that is dragging you down, holding you back, and blocking you from who you were truly destined to be. The message is clear, **we only have one life, make it count.**

Would it not be a wonderful thing to be able to feel that yesterday was for reference and not for residence? The past is where our memories live, and the past can also act as an instructor. Today is the moment that matters. That today is the minutes and moments that we live in, and that tomorrow is where our plans and our dreams live.

To Kat, I hope you are in the arms of angels now and you have found some comfort there. I wish it weren't so, but thank you for being the reason that I finally picked up a pen.

Sharing one's life story is like riding naked on a city bus. You are definitely heading somewhere, but it is an uncomfortable ride. We treasure our secrets and don't relish the idea of having our deepest thoughts laid bare, naked for all the world to see. But truth cares not about our shame or privacy. It demands to be told. So here I am naked. This is my story, my truth, offered as a tribute to those who didn't make it, and a salute to those who did.

Day by day, client by client, one at a time, I live with this hope; That I may help change just one person's direction either away from the doors of addiction hell that I experienced, or just shine a ray of light and hope if they have already arrived there. Perhaps I can give just one person the feeling that if they can find within themselves the courage and strength to seek help, encourage them to seek good professional help to find calm and peace and goodness in their world. If so, then I'm good. If my story can do that, then I'm good, and that's when I'll cry... when that someone again finds life. Not tears of sadness–tears of joy.

To explain how I made it here, I must tell you where it all began. I don't come from a textbook life, although parts of my story read like one. People have often said to me, on hearing about portions of my life, "You've got to share this", and "you need to write a book".

Tell the story of where you came from, who you chose to become, and where you went. Make your story matter, so others don't fall as hard or get help before it's too late.

I can share my truth because I live today in a place of fullness rather than nothingness. The journey to that place was harrowing, traumatic, and required depths of honesty I had never explored before. Once I traversed the dark caverns, though, I saw a faint light in the distance - truth. I followed that light until I stood in the stark radiance of day. That unyielding commitment to truth, within myself first and foremost, has caused the sun to continue to shine on every single beautiful day.

# CHAPTER 2

# *Nasty Realities*

Nasty realities live in my head, compartmentalized and catalogued where they belong. Hidden deep enough so as not to affect my beautiful life, but close enough to drag them out and shame myself in those times when I think for one second about going back to where I came from.

I'm just a kiwi woman in her mid-fifties now, with a dark past. It doesn't define me.  It has made me who I am today, and I'm proud of that. I chose life over the bottle, sparking days, months, and years of making honest amends where amends were due, slowly learning to forgive myself first, and developing the guts to go forth into a life of sobriety. The hardest part was learning to like me, to take care of me, and guard my heart so that I could always be full and present to give love to others. Waiting quietly, patiently, while those who mattered learned to trust me again. Some have forgiven me, some haven't, and that's OK. I understand that we can't turn back time. I accept the things I cannot change now, but I make damn sure I'm loaded with the courage to change the things I can.

I don't blame those I love who struggle with forgiveness. There was a lot to forgive.  Lying came naturally to me for a major part of my life. I have always been a people pleaser. I hate other people feeling uncomfortable; it makes me feel even more uncomfortable. So, when I was young, I learned to lie to please others. I lied to myself a lot, too. That was a big mistake because the lies we tell ourselves are far more potent; doing the greatest amount of damage. But lying was key to my survival, and lying without hurting was how I got by.

Though I was an experienced liar, I wasn't very good at it. The wear and tear of my addiction was starting to creep out into the open. "I'm OK" clearly wasn't one of my best lies. I'd assert that I could handle things when I couldn't. I desperately wanted someone to worry about me.

These days, if someone says to me, "You're lying," I either see purple or the dam bursts. It's a byproduct of my lying days. In March 2014, I put an end to lying. I decided on two options only; tell the truth or I shut up. Silence can truly be golden.

What you read in these pages are the facts and the truth. Certain parties may not see it like that. For example, the New Zealand police might take issue with my version of the truth, Nova Trust Rehab might be another. I respect the police and have worked closely with them since 2015. However, certain individuals need to quit or retire now, as they have lost the ability to separate their opinions from their professional responsibilities. I believe that the base training around understanding mental health and addiction is inadequate, but everyone's hands are tied. The chain that links all services to any decent help for people suffering from Mental Health and/or Addiction issues is broken everywhere in my homeland of New Zealand. As far as Nova Trust in the years 2011/2012 is concerned, I have no desire to attack, but every intention to expose. I am obligated to expose the truth of what they were and the harm they caused so many unwell people who needed someone to see the good in them and offer the professional help that was promised.

All the names of people I talk about are real, but some events that happened in my life will be disguised or left out. I do not seek a platform to air my past differences. Rather, I crave a platform to change the future of others.

# CHAPTER 3

## *Life before my dance with Sav*

I was born in March 1965 in Invercargill, New Zealand, to loving and hard-working parents at a location that the golden arches (Mc Donald's) now proudly claim as home. Both parents were born and raised in Riverton. Our weekends were spent visiting both sets of Grandparents. My father is older than my mother by eight years, so his parents died when I was young, in my pre-teen years.

My father was significantly younger than his three siblings. His father, Alexander, served in World War 1, along with his two brothers, Lionel and George. Though three sons enlisted and went to war, only two returned. My grandfather lived through that war but suffered serious injuries. He spent two years in Ireland at a hospital before finally returning home to New Zealand and Riverton, well after the war had finished. No one ever knew why, only that he had severe lung and leg injuries from shrapnel. He retreated into years of silence following his return.

I am told he loved me most out of his 14 grandchildren, though I don't know why. Perhaps I perceived that he was troubled, sullen even. Or perhaps it was because his knee, where I climbed onto to snuggle close to his chest, was where I was most happy. I suspect the innocent affection of a child distracted him from the horrors his aging eyes had seen. I know I loved my Grandmother, but I have no standout memories of her other than the faint recollection that she was lovely and soft and kind.

My mother's parents were younger, so we spent most of our weekends with them. My mother was an only child, so my two siblings and I were their only grandchildren. Grandad Lindo was an alcoholic, not that I knew it at the time. The struggles he endured silently were unfathomable. My Grandmother had three babies after my Mum was born, but they were all stillborn or died soon after birth. Her RH Negative blood was an almost certain death sentence for them. It was a miracle that my mother survived. In the 1930s, babies who died were discarded literally and figuratively, like they never lived. But we learned in later years that my Grandfather would personally gather each of those discarded babies and have them quietly buried with his late mother.

My mother suffered terribly from the losses as well. Each time expecting a baby brother or sister to come home, not understanding why they didn't. It deeply affected her, as in those days, talking about such great loss was not commonplace. She later became a maternity nurse, much like a modern-day midwife. It may have been a way for her to cope with the losses she experienced. Today, some groups help people of my parent's era, helping them to finally grieve their yesteryear losses. Mum has been to one such group. I'm grateful she can find a place to listen, talk, and possibly receive validation of feelings she had suppressed all those years ago.

The first great loss that I remember happened was when I was 14 years old and my grandfather died suddenly after an operation for lung cancer. I was devastated. I still miss him and wish I had been granted more time with him in my more adult years. I often dream of him still—40 years later. I believe he's always remained around me, maybe there to protect me knowing what might be coming in my life. My dear grandmother went on to live on her own until she died at 94 years old.

As someone who has battled addiction, I often think of my maternal grandfather's alcoholism. Medical science states that 70% of addiction is attributed to genetic predisposition, causing me to wonder if the genes skipped a generation like they are known to, and I became like him. Both of my Grandfathers lived and died without any external or internal understanding of their intense psychological traumas and without any possibility of help like what is offered today.

My sister Robyn was born only 16 months earlier than me with dislocated hips. The day I was born, my grandparents were with Robyn far away in a Dunedin hospital having her first surgery to try and start correcting her condition. Mum knew something was wrong with Robyn's hips as soon as she was born. She was a maternity nurse after all, but nobody listened to her. Instead, she had to wait until Robyn got hurt at around 7 months old. Her injury was enough to warrant an x-ray. Wisely, Mum begged the radiographer to also x-ray her hips.

Thankfully, when my youngest son was born in 1999 with the same condition, I knew a lot about it, having grown up with Robyn. The difference in decades feels like centuries apart.

In 1999, when an orthopaedic Doctor walked into my room to tell me of my son's hip displacement presentation after I had just delivered a breech baby boy we called Jackson by caesarean section, I had a sense of what to expect. Jack was strapped in a tiny full body brace for 6 months; poor Robyn was strapped to a bed for the best part of her first 5 years.

Robyn was and still is tough. She spent years having operation after operation. During her early years, she was always in a plaster cast and rarely lived outside of a hospital ward. Dad built her a trolley to get around on; lying on her belly, she used her arms to push herself where she wanted to go. It was great fun for me to stop her, for all I had to do was put my foot on the front and she wasn't going anywhere. Still, she knew how to hold her own and exact her revenge. When she was sitting up and I was nearby, she would pummel me hard with arms made strong from motoring around under their power. I think I've probably gotten permanent dents in my arm bones where she has landed plenty of paybacks.

It was hard work for both Mum and Dad, juggling between work, me as a young baby, and Robyn always needing to be in Dunedin, which was about 4 hours away from Invercargill. I spent a lot of time in those early days at Mum's cousin's house in the Southern South

Island town of Waimumu. Wendy and Peter loved me like their own. I fondly remember sitting in their kitchen eating sugar sandwiches.

At the age of 30, Robyn was one of the youngest in New Zealand to get a full hip replacement. She has endured two more since then, but continues to take it all in stride. She's tough, she's my sister. I love her dearly and I'm so glad she's mine.

# CHAPTER 4

# *Queenstown*

Queenstown is the home of my soul. The waters of the lake and abundant rivers and streams wash over me whether I am standing in their crystal flows or drinking them in from a distance. The mountains hem me and make me feel safe, towering over me in comfort and protection. I need to immerse myself in mountains and water, now and again still, it grounds me, and so Queenstown is my place to where I often return. Wide open spaces feel good for a while, but I call the mountains and Lake Wakatipu home.

We moved to Queenstown in 1975. Until then, I got to visit the area often, mostly during holidays with my maternal Grandparents, who owned what we mainlanders called "a crib in the camping ground", a South Island term for tiny holiday homes that served as a luxury getaway.

After returning from boarding school, home felt suffocating. I left home and school at 15 years old. I craved freedom, so I spread my wings. Though I was young, I was able to buy myself some wonderful times. I had good friends, great houses to live in, and a really good job. Closing my eyes for even a moment can transport me back to those simple, carefree days. My friends and I were growing up in a safe community inside a small-town atmosphere before the mass development of Queenstown had really started.

It was in that atmosphere that I got my first real exposure to alcohol. Surprisingly, it wasn't a priority for me. I tried weed, but its effects only made me laugh uncontrollably, crave a late-night Jazz Bar Chalky White burger, and promptly fall asleep. I knew immediately that it didn't suit me.

I wasn't a confident girl. I was tall for my age, all legs and arms with no boobs, lacking self-confidence. I was called pretty, but I never really felt I was anything special. I loved affection but didn't really know how to show it, thereby making people assume that I was standoffish, which was the complete opposite of what I felt internally.

"The best and most beautiful things in the
world cannot be seen or even touched
they must be felt with the heart"
*– Helen Keller*

# CHAPTER 5

# *First Loves*

Life changed in 1983 when I met Greg. He exuded kindness, affection, charisma, and charm. For me, it was love at first sight. With him showing me how to love and how to be affectionate, I started to grow into a firm sense of self. I was 18 years old, and he was 28. We were engaged in six months and married six months later. Planned, but still a surprise, I managed to get pregnant right away. By May 1985, when I was just 20, we welcomed our precious newborn son, Joel. Looking into his eyes and experiencing this most perfect pure love, I never anticipated that, 29 years later, it would be this little baby who would ultimately utter the words that would save my life; **"I love you Mum, but I don't want you to ever call me again".**

The marriage didn't last; the age difference was just too great. I wanted to venture further and see the world; Greg was ready to settle down and establish concrete foundations. The distance between us grew, so we tearfully agreed that it was time to go our separate ways. We did then - and still do now - make Joel our number one priority. Despite the brokenness between us, he is the greatest success of our years together. We ensured that, as a toddler, he would not witness arguments or fights. We even went on holiday together throughout his growing years.

Not long after we separated, Greg became gravely ill with a life-threatening lung condition. He would have died if not for a visiting professor from an English medical teaching school who, once presented with the evidence, was able to quickly make a life-saving diagnosis. It worked, and he turned the corner. Still, it was to be a 3 to 4-year recovery, hence the decision for him to return home to Australia where his parents could care for him.

Greg has remained in Australia ever since with his lovely wife, Alex, and her son Max. Over the years, he has been a father to both Joel and Max. Greg is my anchor to this day, a wonderful relationship that his wife Alex graciously allows us. We don't live in each other's countries; our lives are separate. But he is my 'call in emergency' number; in fact, his number is the only number beside my own that I remember by heart. He has been the port in my many bloody storms, and the person that knows by just hearing my voice that I'm either floundering or doing really well. He is my friend. We have never wanted to, nor will we be together again as a couple. But our lives are inextricable. I've promised him I'd wipe the dribble and change his nappy when all is said and done. He is my one degree of separation soul mate, and I love him truly and dearly.

Relationships like this can happen if you decide what's most important. Our focus was on our son's future and how we could stick together to help show him a good path. We remembered what we loved about each other even as we walked away, and we held on to those good memories to keep our connection loving and positive. We aimed high to make our relationship respectful and understanding. In so doing, we gave Joel two parents who loved and grew him together. I was lucky with Alex. She's allowed us our relationship, although, at times, I know she may have felt wounded by it. Greg and I agreed at the beginning of the end of our marriage that we could do this. We believed we could, so we did.

On New Year's Eve 2019, The Lake Conjola bushfires hit without warning. Greg and Alex lost their beautiful family home where Joel and I had many of our happiest memories. That home full of history was gone in minutes. Thankfully, Greg and Alex were OK and out of harm's way. I launched a Go Fund Me page along with Joel, with the hope of raising $2,000. The total amount of donations came to $30,000. It shows you what kind of man I met and married all those years ago. His grace and kindness remain as steady and ever-present today as it has always been.

# CHAPTER 6

# *Digging Holes*

There are huge holes in the story of my upbringing - emotional and psychological holes. I've dug a place to throw them in and bury the sad sorry parts of my life. I'd dragged my chains around for far too long before March 2014. The events of my childhood are not spoken. I don't talk about them because words seem to feed them and make them grow when I have overcome them. I sought expert psychological treatment for the chains that bound me to those traumas, to help free me of their awful heaviness. I dug holes, big ones, and tossed them in. They are dead, buried, and rotting now, serving only as fertilizer for my future. It's not that I want to hide my past, but traumatic events that happened to me were out of my control and are not mine to own anymore. I took care of business where I needed to, and that's enough for me now. Releasing the past was the only way forward for me.

Sometimes you just have to be done; not mad or upset. Just done! It took me a very long time to get to "DONE" on a path I never knew I was walking. When I came to understand what I was doing, I had already sought solace in Sav. The beginning of my self-medicating had long begun.

Getting help, that is the most important thing, raising your hand up, lifting your head up, even just whispering out of your pain, 'I can't do this alone'. Instead, I let the current of addiction sweep me up and carry me further and further away. I was so deep into an addiction to alcohol that I couldn't see my way back to wholeness. Alcohol was my problem, and it was also the answer to my problem. In fact, I thought it was my answer to everything. It wasn't; it was the beginning of the end of everything I truly held dear and loved.

# CHAPTER 7

# *Friendship like rust, it never sleeps-*

The first time I heard the saying, if you can count your true friends, on one hand, you're a blessed person, was from a lovely woman named Shirley Rapley. She was from the generation before mine, the mother-in-law of one of my besties. She witnessed the nature of the friendship that Andi, Tanya, and I had all those years ago and advised us to treasure it. We spent many wonderful days at the home of Shirley and her husband, Frank, sipping warm gin and soda out of marmite jars, listening to the Phantom of the Opera, and drinking in the wisdom of a wise older generation teaching us how to be grateful for what we had.

This was in the early 1980s. By 2011, I had royally fucked up the friendship with these two soul sisters that Shirley warned me to cherish. Conversations and apologies mixed with sadness, grief, and loss ensued before I was able to slowly repair what I had damaged. Three other girls whom I consider part of the sum that makes up the whole of my inner circle are my treasured lifelong friends Nelly, Karen, and Susan. From the age of 13, these five women have, each in their own way, helped direct my path. We have walked through life together, through marriages, divorces, kids, and life's forever unfolding events, and they have a sacred place in my heart. Two of them became godmothers to my sons. We "bridesmaided" each other, we embraced each other through our breakups and held each other up through the grief of love and loved ones lost. They are the second mothers to my children as I am to theirs. Together, we laughed and loved our way through the years.

When I derailed, they tried, separately and together, to rescue me. But all their attempts were unsuccessful. They individually stood by me until, one by one, they could no longer bear the sight of what I had become. In truth, they never really left me; they simply faded into the shadows watching closely but helplessly as the pieces of me slowly fell off.

Today, three of these women are still with me. Though separated by oceans, we live life together as neighbours. While I sit out the COVID-19 pandemic in the northern ancient city of Chiang Mai as well as the Southern Islands of Thailand, they carry on their lives in New Zealand.

Susan was diagnosed with cancer in December 2013 at the age of 59. I wasn't sober when she found out and called me, so I did what my dysfunction dictated; I made a big deal about it being all about me. There are so many things I gained from finally choosing life over the bottle, but this one stands out in the forefront; I was sober when she died.

The last time I saw her was 2 weeks before her death. We sat together at my parent's house in Dunedin. Susan talked about what she had planned for her big day (her funeral), and I started to tear up while trying so hard not to. Susan didn't want tears.  But she also knew me so well. She spoke these words:

> *Girly, don't you bloody dare use my death*
> *as your excuse to go back to where you have*
> *come from. Don't you bloody dare. You don't*
> *belong there and if you did go back, you'd be*
> *joining me, and I don't want you to join me.*

I often think of her and look up knowing that she is looking back at me. I thank her for teaching me to be strong and telling me not to retreat back into addiction. On that June day in 2014, I was just three months sober, but since then I have not allowed anyone's actions or looked within mine to find and use as an excuse to go back to where I came from. Her parting message has never left me; I've carried it with me all these years, and when I need to remind myself of how far I've come, I think of Susan and her last words to me. Many times, I've shared those powerfully motivating final words with others when they were struggling too. **No. Bloody. Excuses**. I want her to know that I listened to her. Sometimes I feel her around, she sends me little messages like a feather dropping at my feet, and then I know she knows.

As our time together neared the end, I drove her back to the place she was staying near the hospital. We locked eyes, gave each other the finger, and said, well fuck off then. She lost her voice soon after that day, so I never heard her speak again. But the words she left me with the last time she spoke to me were potent enough to last a lifetime. She died peacefully, her way, ten days later. That was the closing curtain of 33 years of a bloody funny, honest, faithful, beautiful friendship I was so blessed to have.

My friends and family were so worried I would immediately return to my old normal when Susan died that they waited until the next morning when they knew I was at an outpatients' meeting in a rehab to call and tell me she was gone.

Susan's death set the stage for my first big challenge; coping with adversity while remaining sober. Do I, or don't I? I chose *don't*. Simple! I surrounded myself with people who cared. I kept my promise to Susan, and I didn't make her death an excuse. Instead, I went home and poured all my love, memories, and tears into knitting a beanie.

It was at Susan's party (as she wanted it to be called) that Andi walked back into my life. Seconds after seeing each other, we let go of past hurts, embraced, and loved each other again. In an instant, we reverted to besties. Andi's words were as powerful as Susan's;

*I'm so sorry, I just couldn't handle what was
happening to you, so I had to stand back.*

I assured her that I couldn't stand being with me either, so I understood how she felt. Five years after I got my dear friend Andi back, she was diagnosed with cancer at the age of 57. She didn't want to leave and fought so hard to stay. She left in January 2018.

Andi's diagnosis and the times during her illness brought Tanya back into my world. It had always been the three of us in a beautiful friendship born years before. And it was my actions that pushed Andi and Tanya into the dark.

The old phrase, "two's company and three is a crowd" didn't apply in our circle; however, Andi and Tanya shared an extra special bond. They thought the same way but acted it out differently with their own individual personalities. I loved them equally and was never jealous of what they had. I was just so bloody thankful they had it, especially in the end when Tanya flew from Perth to Queenstown regularly to just 'sit and be' with our beautiful friend in her last days, and with that, a time that we were able to acknowledge and cherish our 38 years of unconditional friendship.

To say it was unfair that Andi got the big C is wasted grief, but in Andi's case, it's worth saying that she was one of the fittest women I knew. She biked up mountains after work, even biking through Vietnam a year earlier. She went on kilometer-long hikes into the hills around her, worked for years at gyms, and was a conscious eater long before *vegan* and *vegetarian* were common words. She didn't know that a constantly bloated stomach was a sign of ovarian cancer. Because she was so fit, they could medically throw the works at her; and they did. In a small window of a hopeful period, she and her husband, Beau, set off travelling around Europe for 6 months.

On her return from Europe, they passed through Bangkok. One of those universal moments happened when I discovered that I was booked on the same flight home as them. Andi wasn't well; she felt she had picked up the flu in Dubai. Although she wouldn't say so, I could see it was clearly worrying her. She was tired and, in a way, the words she spoke reflected this. She told me she wanted to go home and make sure she "made time for herself now."

Andi told me she knew she wouldn't make old bones but hoped that she would live to see 65. I'll never forget those epic words: "make time for me now." I believe everyone has got to make time for themselves now, before an illness or a challenge. Don't wait; don't always put others first; make time for you now. I make 'me' time a priority these days. It's not selfish, it's a mainstay for my mental and physical health. If I don't make 'me' matter, I'm a bit buggered really, and it will often show in my inability to cope with the smallest of things. It will show when I am not being fully present with the people who matter most and deserve my full attention.

Another profound and deeply moving statement Andi made while on that long flight back to our motherland was:

> *Denise, you and I have both got an illness—a*
> *disease. The only difference is, what I have is*
> *recognized, and people run forward to help me,*
> *while you, on the other hand, have a disease*
> *that is not recognized. It's so misunderstood*
> *that people run the other way, leaving you to*
> *battle it alone. Both of them can kill us, but*
> *mine is seen as a strength in the fight, whereas*
> *yours is seen as a weakness in a battle that*
> *you could have avoided to begin with.*

That's my oldest, dearest, most kind, and gracious friend, Andi. She really did always see things from both sides.

I spend a lot of time in other people's worlds, worlds that are full of life-strangling issues. It's easy to get caught up in other people's pain and forget about self-care. So, focusing on me first enables me to be more present to help others. Often, I may have back-to-back clients, once needing to travel between New Zealand and Thailand three times in three weeks. While my schedule was so suffocating, I barely got any "me" time at all other than a quiet moment at the airport and on the flights home to collect another client. Three times in three weeks, I actually walked into glass sliding doors. The fatigue had something to do with it, but overall, little bits of 'me' were everywhere, and 'me' time had been neglected. I have learned to put myself first, not selfishly, but lovingly so that I have plenty to give to those who need me.

"You have brains in your head. You have feet in your shoes. You can steer yourself any direction you choose" – *Dr Seuss*

CHAPTER 8

# *Building a Career*

I was always quite normal, whatever the hell that is—nothing outstanding, nothing special, just a young woman who had wonderful family and friends and good relationships with a wide group of people. I worked hard while I continued to grow up with my young son.

I lived in Queenstown for 34 years before moving with my second husband and two younger children to Wellington in 2009. I always had a job, starting with the Queenstown Telephone Exchange (only the over 40s would know what that is) working in tourism with rafting, jet boating, and bungy companies. I had my bus license and drove buses into Skipper's Canyon and up the mountains for ski transport. I worked at restaurants, bars, a florist shop, shoe shops, fashion stores, and jewellers. I regularly modelled clothes in fashion shows along with a weekly stint on the catwalk every Sunday at O'Connell's, which was Queenstown's only shopping mall back then.

The very first big moment of believing I could achieve something great happened in 1991. I auditioned for TV commercials and crowd scenes in films that had taken off around the Wakatipu Basin and Southern Lakes area. I was rarely successful in securing roles as my lack of confidence and self-esteem came screaming through the lens of the camera. I did, however, land a role that was to change the direction of my working career.

A movie called the *Brotherhood of the Rose* was shooting in the Fiordland area with its main star, Robert Mitchum. He was an oldie but a goodie, although I could tell that alcohol played a leading role in his daily life. The movie was shot partly around Fiordland with my extra part being a non-speaking, high-class hooker. It took two weeks to film. All I had to do was lean over the shoulder of the mafia boss and walk through or sit down in numerous scenes. I nearly died when I was picked along with five others for the roles of flashy working girls. It was my hair and its color that landed me the job. Along with the great money I was earning, I loved being a part of it all. But the experience confirmed to me that I bloody hated being in front of a camera.

I spent a lot of time talking with a woman who oversaw the extra talent and slowly started building a picture of what was required to do work behind the scenes (and behind the camera) in the film industry.

On returning home, I sat down and talked to my bestie and the fourth of my dear friends I can count on one hand, Nelly. I said, "Why not start a Casting Company?" so that is precisely what we did. 'Southern Scenes Casting' was born and later became a talent agency that Nelly ran along with Karen. I continued as a Casting Director for more than 20 years.

Barbara Williams of 'Shoot NZ' gave us our first job two weeks after we started advertising our company—a venture we really didn't have a clue how to run. We gathered friends who had already gotten their foot in the door of the film industry, learned how to use a camera with the help of a friend, then took what I knew from all my mostly unsuccessful auditions, and the rest is history.

Wow! Those were the days. It was exciting—especially in the early times. Both Nelly and I had no interest in the crew scene of the film industry. We simply loved the job, the travel, and the people we met. Every day, people had their lives changed with one TV commercial or film role. Whether it was working as an extra or a featured talent part, the money was huge and had the power to change people's lives overnight.

There were so many wonderful moments from those times. To call and tell a single, struggling mother of 3 beautiful children that they had all been chosen for a role in a commercial that paid more than she could possibly earn in 2 years were moments I lived for. Firstly, the mum was so excited that they all had the role. She didn't ask or think about the money. She just hoped it would cover the rent and food for next week. Oh, the joy of being a part of making success happen for people was exhilarating.

We got to travel New Zealand and the world with 'Southern Scenes' meeting big-name actors and working with amazing people in the production teams, along with being part of successful movies like 'The World's fastest Indian." But nothing stands out more from those times than the people I would meet and audition. I possessed the art of communication already. I may not have had the confidence to put myself on television, but my ability to easily talk to people was in my bones. I like people, always have. I am interested in them to the point that I would describe people as my hobby. My son Joel and my eldest daughter both went on to work behind and in front of the camera and still do so successfully to this day.

My last job in my career was in 2010. I had recently moved to Wellington and was asked to do a job for a production company whose name I've forgotten and for a commercial brand that doesn't matter. I only recall parts of the job, flying to Queenstown and auditioning people in total blackout. Apparently, I flew from Queenstown to Brisbane to drop work off at the production company, but that's all a blur. I do remember coming home with a really nice pair of boots from the trip. Those boots lived a life of solitude in the back of the wardrobe never to be worn due to what they reminded me of. They did make excellent wine holders for a time, however.

The production company couldn't use the casting auditions I had delivered, which came as no surprise. I knew by then that my life as a Casting Director in the industry was over. I never auditioned another soul after that job. My light was going out, and the only glow in my life was the one beckoning me toward another glass of Sav.

Another important part of my formative years was the Gin Club. In fact, this was the era that preceded the great change that happened shortly thereafter. As the name reflects, the Gin Club involved alcohol - Gin to start with. But it included whatever liquid rocked our boat as the girls gathered every Friday night to drink and socialize. It had been started by a group of women who all worked at Shotover Jet, back in the day when it was only a caravan for an office perched on the hill above the Shotover River in Arthur's Point, Queenstown, long before the days of corporate ownership. I was employed there before my brilliant idea to tap into a career in the film industry. They truly were some of the happiest days of my twenties. Jim and Karen Boult had only just taken over the ownership of Shotover Jet from Heather and Trevor Gamble, who had made it a success up until that time.

Jim was a lovely man, feared slightly by us girls in the office, but a good man. We had handheld radios and a great viewpoint to see when his vehicle was coming over the Edith Cavell bridge, so we would quickly radio to let our small team know he was on his way. Many years later, he told me he also had a radio that he turned on as he was nearing the base, so he could hear our frantic warning of his arrival. He also told me he knew my 4-year-old son Joel was being hidden in the second caravan on occasion when childcare failed, and I needed to bring him to work. He never said a word about it at the time. Hats off and much respect to you, Jim.

The Gin Club started in the caravan in the early 90s but ended years later. Most Friday nights were spent at my house mainly due to its central location. The girls moved on to different jobs, married, had babies, and grew older. One thing that didn't change in those years with any of us was Friday night Gin Club, no boys allowed. Between 5 pm and 8 pm, it was girl's time. Any man new to a relationship with any of us quickly learned to accept it. How lucky I was to have that group of friends! As life unfolded, each of us would listen and talk over glasses of wine about our joys or woes. Nothing left the Gin Club unsolved or without at least a good idea of how to fix your shit.

The same tight group remained for years, though some came and went as they moved into town or out of town. But a solid core of 6 of us remained for years. Our young children were also very much a part of the infamous Friday evenings. I think they knew and loved the fact that there was always a lot of laughter, their Mums were happy, they were allowed chips, lollies, and fizzy which wasn't common, along with being lectured on how to treat a woman. Joel still refers to his growing years with the Gin Club girls as to where he first learned that women are special and should be treated with respect and care.

The final Fridays of Gin Club gatherings came to an end when, all at once, three girls who were my close friends moved on. Adele and Kathi finally left Queenstown and Jilly chose to end her own life and leave this world.

It's still with such sadness that I acknowledge that even now, nearly 24 years later. I don't want to speculate or debate suicidal matters; I have my own thoughts surrounding it. I do know that even one death is not acceptable. New Zealand has one of the highest suicide rates amongst our young people in the modern world per capita. What can I do or say?

I am not stating that suicide and addiction always go hand in hand, but addiction can either come from depression and it always leads to depression 100% of the time. Alcohol and drugs are depressants, so what I do in helping people, I do one person at a time.

What I do know is if we had a better understanding of depression, she may have lived. Gin Club wasn't enough for her; although we were her port, our clearly diminishing Friday night numbers and her close friends leaving must have made her feel even more alone–more alone than where she already lived inside her head.

We took Jilly to a doctor three days before she left this earth. He prescribed her antidepressants, but with no warning to us that she might plunge further and harder into depression in the first few weeks before she would feel better and start to pick up. This combined with my knowledge now, that drinking casks full of wine stopped any chances of her medication working, while the alcohol only made her more depressed and created more anxiety than already was part of her world, leaves me feeling sad that she never got the chance to get the help she needed.

I didn't know the signs of suicide ideation then; the presentation of a person whose decision to die had been made and was just waiting for the right time to execute it. When she came to my home that morning, on the day that she left us, she seemed happier and more at peace than she had been in a very long while. Perhaps it was the knowledge that her suffering would end that day that left her awash in contentment and disconnected from the pain she'd leave us all to carry and the future she would never enjoy. However, for the first time ever, she left me with a look over her shoulder and a wave, instead of her trademark hugs and kisses. She oozed affection, love, and cared for everyone, with none left in the pot for herself.

Connection and love do make the world go around; it's just sometimes not enough for some whose pain is too great to stay.

"While we try to teach our children all about life, Our children teach us what life is all about" – *Angela Schwindt*

# CHAPTER 9

# *Children of the Heart*

In 1996, I was gifted with the love of a 3-year-old girl. She returned my motherlove. My love for her brother and sister followed a little while later but to begin with, it was this little toddler that captured my heart first.

One morning, I heard a noise at my door. All I could see was the top of a pink barbie helmet with a barbie bike lying on the lawn. When I opened the door, this sweet-faced angel was asking if she could come and play with me. All would have been well, except there was no adult attached to her. She had made her way to me from 800 meters away from her Grandparents' house to mine. I'd started dating her father a month earlier, and, as this wee one wasn't at school yet, I saw her nearly every other day.

For different reasons, her father and I were keeping our very fresh relationship under wraps, therefore I had little to do with the other 2 children, aged 7 and 8 years old. After the wee one made that daring escape to my house that morning, it quickly became clear to us that the secret relationship wasn't so secret after all.

This man and his children would be an integral part of the next 16 years of my life.

They say blood is thicker than water and sometimes it's true, sometimes it isn't. In my case, it was not. I was gifted these 3 beautiful children who I refer to as being born from my heart. I raised them like they were my blood. In 1999, little Jackson was born, making us a family of 7, with 5 very individual and beautiful children. As parents, neither my husband nor I referred to our children as stepsons or stepdaughters. He referred to Joel as his son, and I referenced his children as my sons and daughters. The children have always used the term "brother" and "sister." It makes me want to leak a happy tear when I see them all together these days behaving as siblings—as family. It's rare to get them all in one place because they are spread out over the globe. But, now and again, it happens, and when it does, my heart soars.

In the early days of life with him, I was happy. I so loved our large family. Not only did we have our 5, but they each had 5 or so close friends. The house was constantly filled with children, filled with conversation, and filled with laughter. I moved my casting studio into our renovated garage and continued to work from there. Days ticked by with me slowly beginning to forget that I only kept remnants of yogurt and milk in my fridge at my home; a local restaurant called "The Moa" was mine and Joel's kitchen. I wanted this life, and I was fulfilled and happy.

There were so many moments that made my old life seem empty in comparison to the new. There were so many opportunities to make a difference, shape their lives, and show them love. The first time our middle son climbed up onto my knee, he pretty much stayed there till he was around twelve years old. The wee one got teased at Kindergarten about saying she had two mothers, so the teacher arranged for three of her friends to accompany her and me to the cemetery and explain that she has a mother in heaven and a mother here on earth. And once the older daughter really started allowing me in, needing me, slowly but surely a beautiful bond was formed. Joel slowly got used to being a big brother to three younger siblings in stark contrast to his life as an only child at ten years old. This was a huge adjustment, but he grew up well and happy with plenty of noise in his childhood.

Our youngest, Jackson, landed himself in this world with six parents rather than two. The wee one despised him from the start for not being a girl. She called him "it" for the first year, and constantly tried to nudge him out of my arms while I was feeding him in her fight for full ownership of me. His first word being a baby version of her name was priceless, making her give in to loving him forever.

I never wanted to take the place of the mother they had lost, so when the wee one asked if she could call me Mummy, I carefully explained that her other Mummy in heaven owned that name, and maybe she could give me her own special title. "Neecie" was really born then and stuck. It's one nickname I rarely get called these days, and I miss it.

Now and again I get a phone call from my children with a need that can only be met by me. After all those years of placing motherhood first, I still need to be present in their lives to help them and not be in motherhood retirement. So, when it happens, my mother heart quickly fills up and is replenished.

I do not share the names of the three children I raised from my heart because I loved them first as I love them now. I have always wanted to protect them, so I leave out pieces that would have an impact on them. We may be oceans apart now, physically, and some-times emotionally. But I am forever indebted to them for the love they showed me through those times. I own my decline. I know it wasn't easy for them to watch or be a part of, and for that, I will be forever sorry. To them I say:

*Thank you for letting me love you. Thank you, wee one, for taking that big adventure and making it to my front door.*

My husband doesn't have a name because *he* doesn't matter. I haven't really used it for years. Most memories I have of those 16 years with him are gone. I find it hard to conjure them up, so I just don't. There is no emotion, no hurt, and no happiness. There is just space. The good memories started to fade when pieces of our marriage began breaking down. It's long gone now, and there is nothing left but a hole where 16 years of my life with him disappeared.

I treasure the memories I have of raising our children. There were many beautiful moments. I hold the same love for each of them today as I did when I met them all those years ago. I've done all I can, where I can, to make amends for the moments that were not good. I don't need to be forgiven as such; I just want them to live their lives without resentment. I want them to be happy, to be loved, and to have calm and peace in their world. That's enough for me.

# CHAPTER 10

## *Panic!*

My first panic attack happened in the New World supermarket in Cromwell.

I had no idea what the hell was happening to me, except that I was spinning, my chest was pumping like mad, and I was finding it hard to breathe. I was purchasing water, so I grabbed it and threw half of it over me. Either the cold water or the embarrassment of my action had an effect, as within a few minutes it passed, and I started to feel normal again. I was around 34 years old.

They say anxiety or panic attacks are common in places like the supermarket, or while driving places where you feel trapped and can't quickly get away. I did not know about this back then. Anxiety was not a word I used. To be honest, I thought people who complained of anxiety needed to toughen up, get a grip, and handle it. Stressed out was ok, but suffering from anxiety, yeah… nah. Little did I know that chronic anxiety had lived within me for years. I'd just inanely learned to redirect it, putting masks on to cover how I really felt. So many masks, that the true me just didn't really exist. Not yet anyway.

I was never prone to go to a doctor; I still don't. That's what Google is for. I researched the symptoms which gave me an idea of what may have happened. Also, I told my dear friend, Susan, who was a nurse what happened and then pretty much forgot about it. I wasn't having a heart attack, so I pushed it aside and I got on with life. Until it happened again…

My days were madness. I don't have to break down what raising five children looks like. You can guess, I'm sure. Truth be known, I thought I was capable of anything, a veritable superwoman! Along with almost full-time work in casting, we also built and turned studio apartments on our land into nightly accommodations. We purchased the house next door and did the same with that. As if that wasn't enough, we also had Japanese exchange students living with us which the kids loved.

Some days when I was casting, I would find myself trying to accidentally audition people for a butter commercial when all they wanted was to check into their accommodation. Most days, I had three sets of different dinners I'd make on the go while flying around trying to cast a job. Between dropping off and picking up from dawn to dusk, I didn't stop. And I loved it. I loved it because others were taken care of, everyone was growing up healthy and happy, plus the bonus was that I knew by wine o'clock, I could open a nice cold Sav and bloody well finally breathe. Simple as that.

We were a social couple, *him,* and me. Because our house was large and in the centre of town, we had drop-ins all the time. Weekends were often barbeques at our house with all kids welcome. Long weekends were usually spent at our holiday home near Riverton at a place called Colac Bay. Nelly and I had purchased the house a few years early for a getaway house, just before *he* and I got together, but really our large family took over the place, making it more sensible for us to buy Nelly out. They were good times and wonderful memories made there. We lost that lovely house to fire caused by idiots that had used it for a few nights' stay. We eventually moved another house from Riverton onto the land that ironically was built and lived in by my father's side of the family from yesteryear.

Almost all my friends would say they had never really seen me drunk until I hit my late 30s. I always drank a bottle of wine, but I did slowly enough that it was not noticeable. I would start at 5ish or a little earlier if I had no driving to do, and I'd stop around the time I sat down to eat the third sitting of dinners I'd made. Much later when I looked back, I could see I began as a classic, extremely high functioning lover of fine wines—if only the high functioning part had lasted. But it did not. Like any good thing, too much of it will eventually turn around and bite you in the bum.

My wine was my friend. I laughed, I sang, and I danced with her, and I could breathe when I drank wine. People used to comment or joke about how I could possibly live as I did with so much constantly on my plate. I'd just smile and say, "Nothing a good Sav won't fix." My parents thought it was all too much; the family, the job, the nightly accommodation. My mother would tell me to slow down, but I ignored her.  In fact, when anyone suggested I was overscheduled, I'd get offended and in return turn it up a notch, find something else to throw into my day and into the chaos I was personally creating for myself. I really thought I could cope, but I couldn't. I didn't cope.  It's just that I was crumbling too slowly for anyone to notice. It was too late to reverse out of the life I found myself living, even if I wanted to. I was drowning my problems, little by little, but as I was to discover later, problems were bloody good swimmers.

It's no wonder, in hindsight, that my inner tension spilled over in the form of panic attacks that increased as my life got busier. I somehow got used to them, and I knew that when the dusk hours came to rescue me, I could get together with my dear friend Sav and drink the tightness away.

To put a month and a year on when it all started to break is hard. Even now, it just all seems to run into one long horror movie for me. I knew by 2006 I was in trouble. Highly functioning, but in trouble.

Certain things out of my control happened and opened a huge crack. I told no one of the panic I was starting to feel all the time. I didn't want to look like I couldn't do this life, like I couldn't handle it all. I couldn't let anyone in, and I couldn't get anything out. So Sav started to turn from a good time friend into a numbing agent.

Being told that I had to control it felt like a threat. To stop drinking every day, slow down to weekends only, even worse, quitting all together seemed impossible, but I couldn't admit it.

I take ownership of this, 100 percent. I had started to slip in the way I drank. As I was getting older and the panic became more gripping, I felt myself continuing to get worse.  My behavior and presentation while drinking turned bizarre. I looked and sounded drunk like I hadn't before. I'd make stupid comments, fall over, embarrass myself, and embarrass others around me. I started taking on a morbid stance around death which culminated with me finding something to cry about. I'd embarrass my kids in front of their friends, and I'd try to be one of their group, especially the older two. When this was pointed out to me the next day after a binge, I'd shrink into a corner or try and defend myself while knowing they were right. Though I couldn't recall it, I knew I'd done something ridiculously stupid around them and their friends.

I was trapped. I started to really not like who I had become. I didn't like *him* anymore either. I knew wine was the answer and my only saving grace to the chaos of my daily life, and more importantly, the only way I knew how to get some reprieve from my inner turmoil and pain. *He* lived in a glass house and was throwing huge boulders at me by trying to tell me to stop. My core was taking a bashing. Once you start hearing the words, "You're an alcoholic," that dirty, bloody truth of it strikes at the heart, and any other name I was known by dimmed in comparison.

I was so done and so tired of fighting about it, I took the only course of action I knew; I hid it. There were times when I stopped in the early days. I could go for a week or ten days white knuckling it, hating every second I couldn't drink. I'd go through stages of being angry or just turn completely inside of myself. I tried hard not to let the kids see that anything was wrong with me, but it was clear to all around me that I was coming unglued.

I went to see an Alcohol and other Drug (AOD) counselor at Thorpe House in Christchurch. Thankfully, it was up to me to go and sort myself out, so I was able to drink over the few days I went there. I completed a test where she asked questions about how much, how long, etc. I lied, and I ticked off what I hoped was my last encounter with the dark side of my affair with Sav. She told me I had a problem, NO SHIT, and then I came home and took Jackson off to the south coast for a five-day non-drinking stint. I found that I could do those sober breaks away. Quiet and calm times with no one looking at me seemed to make it easier, then.

I continued to function on the home and work level by finding ways to drink without anyone knowing or seeing. It's a standard way that most people with a substance issue get around being able to continue what they are addicted to. This is when it all takes a serious turn for the worse. I had to drink fast, I had to pretend that I hadn't, and I had to lie and lie more often. No longer for the reasons that I lied before, now it was to protect my wine and my dependence on it. I was spiraling further down and more out of control emotionally, psychologically, becoming chemically addicted, and I wasn't stopping.

It was like I was living two or three different lives. One was a mother who made sure all the children's needs were taken care of, clothes were washed, sports, friends, school, repeat, repeat, repeat. I continued to work and work well with all my casting jobs and nightly accommodation. Then I'd switch out to a new persona when no one could see me, and I'd drink like a fish till I was pleasantly numb. Then I'd wake up in the early morning, being the closest version of the real me I knew, and I'd lie there with sickening thoughts and a realization of what I'd done and who I'd become.

Finding enough time to do this wasn't hard either. *He* had taken up multi-sports a few years earlier and was rarely around. Between the company we owned and that, *he* was absent 70 % of the time.

With the move to Wellington in 2009, I thought that I, and the way things were could really change. For a period, we were happy again, or I thought we were. My drinking slowed, and I seemed to regain some control of my panic. Three of the five children had left home to venture forth and start forging their own paths.

I don't know when and I don't know how, but things turned to crap again. I do know that addiction to a substance can lie dormant and fool you into believing you don't really have an addiction at all.

Into the second year in Wellington, I felt things beginning to break again in terms of my marriage along with my ability to control the amount I drank. I started hiding it again, but this time it was different; it started to scare me how much it was controlling me and how much I now really needed it to be even somewhat functional - let alone happy. My GP was able to arrange a place in a Rehab, so I agreed to try it.

I found myself in a Detox bed in the Medical ward of a hospital about a week later. From there I went directly into a 9-week private rehab facility that was run by a trust in the Lower Hutt area.

Surprisingly, I loved it, not because I learned anything (I really didn't). We went from the 5-bedroom house (rehab house) in Waterloo, to a CADS (Community Alcohol and Drugs Services) group four days a week with one private therapy session thrown in for good measure. We talked about what drugs and alcohol did to us and how different substances did different things to our brains. About the well mind and unwell mind, the 'why' we did it, to begin with, wasn't questioned. We explored the genetic deposition and how addictive tendencies can be passed every second generation. We even covered social , economic and environmental effects, but we weren't taken into a room with a professional and asked why we needed to be numb in the first place, or what happened that left us so fragmented that we wanted to rely on a substance to feel ok. The 'why' didn't matter?

What I loved about it was that, for the first time in almost fifteen years, it was just me. Nine long wonderful weeks of just me. I loved being sober; I loved eating and sleeping well. But most of all, for the first time in years, I didn't have to think about anyone. I could just be myself.

My parents had flown up to look after the youngest one while *he* just carried on with work and multi-sports training, so, everyone seemed happy.

It was in my first ever private therapy session that I began to understand my anxiety. I denied it, made excuses for it, told the therapist she didn't really see the big picture clearly, but the answer was as clear then as it is now. I clearly had a lot of anxiety that caused massive debilitating panic attacks. The more I drank, the more I fed my anxiety, and alcohol created anxiety on top of anxiety, causing me to feed myself an unhealthy double dose of anxiety. There was not the time, or it was not the place, but to start to question deeper issues along with why I carried so much inner anxiety may have helped.

At the end of that nine-week program there was one last meeting with the therapist whose words to *him* and I were, "Take time for you now". Don't go directly to work. Slow down and make yourself important. That happened on Friday, and on Monday, I went back to work in our company against the advice of the therapist. I'd had my nine weeks to get fixed, so it was time to get back into action again. It proved to be a mistake.

Within two weeks, I was drinking, slowly to start, but it increased with time. I'd stop at Pak-n-Sav that was conveniently located next to the train station as I made my way home. I'd hide in the toilets and knock back two or three mini bottles of wine. The first time was with no thought as to why, but it was with plenty of acknowledgment of where this was heading, soon after.

*"Hullo there Sav, my old friend. I've
come to dance with you once again"*

There was really no excuse I could use to explain why I needed it again. The panic attacks had subsided as I was still basking in the memory and feeling of 'me' time. I just did it because I could.

Psychologically speaking, once you have an addiction to a substance, it never really goes away; it just hides in the shadows waiting for when you need or want to let it ignite again. I was no longer chemically addicted; however, I was most certainly mentally addicted to finding peace and calm in a bottle. It owned me, and I let it.

Alcoholism, like drug addiction, is a progressive disease that, if not treated correctly, will only continue to get worse. Just like any addictive substance, it will physically damage you from the inside out. Fact is, when you stop and start again, your liver and mind remember, so it reverts to the damage you did last time and carries on from there. You indeed pick up from where you left off with your last drink, quickly! One is too many, and a thousand is not enough.

People who either suffer from Substance Use Disorder (SUD) or known as Substance Abuse Disorder (SAD) in some countries, or those who are around them watching this sad, sorry show unravel, will know that no matter how many times an addict stops when they start again, the physical and mental presentation will deteriorate at a really rapid rate.

I personally know many people who have died within days of relapsing after two years of sobriety, and I know people who are hospitalized with eminent organ failure within hours of throwing back that beloved Vodka bottle for the first time in months. It's the same with drugs; overdose is common with the first relapse. You may think you can go back to what and how much you were doing before. Sadly, our organs are not equipped to handle this; the shock is so great, they just give up and shut you down to die.

For me, things went south to 'uglyville' very quickly after I started visiting the Pak-and-Sav supermarket toilets in the last months of 2010.

I'd agreed to take Antabuse, a lovely medication that is taken daily and causes an immediate reaction to any alcohol consumed. The reaction can be as extreme as a cardiac arrest, or if alcohol was present in your body, you could experience the onset of symptoms like turning bright red along with your heart going a lot faster than it's meant to. It's a great deterrent for some, and I don't hold an opinion on any course you take to stop drinking. It's just that this medication is not enough to overcome the psychological reasons you started to rely on a substance, to begin with, or learn to live a good life after addiction.

In the times that I really tried hard not to drink, I'd allow *him* to give me this concoction with the knowledge that alcohol was truly off the shopping list for at least 48 hours, until the medication had passed through my system.

My unwell mind got cleverer. After several weeks of this, I decided sobriety wasn't for me. The medication looked like aspirin when dissolved in a glass of water, so instead of *him* giving it to me at 5:30 am when we would wake up, I'd get up earlier, mix up an aspirin, then wander around with it until he woke up, and finish the last of it off in front of him. I knew he counted the tablets, so I'd already discarded them in the garden. One time he challenged me about my self-medicating, so I offered him the glass of dissolved aspirin and told him to try it if he didn't believe me. Not wanting to experience the effects of a heart attack when he had a beer was enough for me to get away with that little routine for a while.

Another way that my unwell mind played games was to move the hiding places all the time. The wine bottle as a boot support was too easy, so I had to up my game. The garden was a short-lived hiding place, whereas the dirty laundry basket lasted quite a bit longer. The cistern in the toilet played out well for a bit, and then I tried the engine of my car. One brainstorm moment I had was with vodka in a hot water bottle, but the taste of rubber soon put an end to that. Eventually, all were discovered, so I just had to keep coming up with more and more interesting and imaginative places.

Believe me, those who suffer from addiction are bloody smart. It gets confused with intelligence sometimes, high IQ; it's not, it's just bloody smart. They are highly motivated to go to any lengths possible to protect the one thing that an unwell mind and chemically dependent body are demanding. One step ahead of the clear and present danger of that substance being taken away from you.

It doesn't just stop with substances either; it extends to anything that a person can become addicted to. The chemicals and neurotransmitters in the brain operate in the same wave pattern for any addiction a person may have, good or bad. The effects of dopamine on our brains should be taught in schools. It's that important to understand.

I started going to AA meetings, which I enjoyed. A kind man, whose name I have forgotten but who belongs to a long list of people who tried to help me, picked me up and drove me to meetings. One meeting resonates with me due to the speaker that night. The woman who spoke had a beautiful voice with a graceful appearance of beauty for her age. Her story shocked me. She spoke of where she had come from and who she was before alcoholism stole her. Her story sounded like mine until she spoke of what alcoholism led her to do. That's when the comparison stopped. It was a shock hearing what she'd done and seeing two completely different pictures of a person. I remember arrogantly saying to myself, "Really? I'm never going to become you." It only took another three years before I caught a glance of myself in a mirror and realized I was her.

I spent Christmas Day 2010 drinking wine that I stored in the laundry cupboard, downing half the bottle at once, and then floating around pretending to be sober. I know I didn't fool *him*, and I do believe that too much wine had flowed between us for *him* to keep fighting me and my Sav anyway. Again, I take full ownership of that.

On Boxing Day 2010, I got a phone call from my family that my 94-year-old Grandmother had suffered a stroke and was not expected to live. My first thought was to get to her side as fast as I could. However, my second thought as I packed to leave and fly to Invercargill was, 'Christ I've got an opportunity to drink'. So, I did.

By the time my flight touched down in Invercargill and I stumbled out of the plane, my father's first words to me were not a warm greeting. Instead, he said, "Christ, how could you? You're drunk". For any normal human in a normal world, you'd think that staying sober, not only out of respect for your dearly loved Grandmother, but also for your grieving mother and family members would be enough of a motivation. It wasn't; alcoholism owned me by now, I didn't function unless I used it. Physically, I was starting to need it to operate on all levels of day to day life. I needed it just to be able to hold my Grandmother's hand through those few nights. I watched her slowly leave this world while I slowly sipped on wine.

I was still able to get a job done and done well at this stage as long as I had wine in my bloodstream. I was able to play a decent role in arranging her funeral that was held the day she died. On the 31st of December 2010, we buried my Grandmother with her beloved husband and my beautiful Grandfather who had died years ago. They were finally together again. Then I stumbled back onto a plane and went home.

My actions around my Grandmother's death had a profound effect on me after that last week of December. The shame I felt far exceeded any other wrongs I had done to date. My choice to drink openly around her dying and death went a lot deeper than all the other horrible things I had done. I went home disgusted with who I was—self-respect at an all-time low.

Due to this, I upped the ante on trying to help others. It's another quite common presentation of a person who suffers from

SUD or other mental health issues: going out of their way to try and pour everything they have into trying to help other people. Because addicts are incapable of helping themselves, they try hard to help others so they can feel better. Just one of the many vicious cycles that most people go through when they are so unwell themselves.

I got back in touch with people who I'd been to rehab with, because, you know, they really understood me. They didn't! How could they? I didn't understand myself. I tried to help those who had fallen over, even supporting someone financially to cover a power bill or whatever. Nothing really helped them just as nothing helped me. For different reasons, we were all in the same washing machine—just on different cycles.

I was charged with drunk driving around this time. Thankfully, some motorist noticed that I was driving wildly on the motorway and called the police. By the time they caught up with me, I was almost home. I knew I was in it up to my eyeballs as I could see a van following me off the motorway and around the back streets toward home. I was taken to the police station where I quietly took what was coming to me. I knew it had been coming for a long time and now that it was here, I was relieved. Once I'd been processed, I left, walked over to the supermarket, got more wine, drank it, caught a bus home, got the spare keys, and walked 600 meters up the road to my car and brought it home. Shameful horror, that was me 100%. It kept me from getting behind the wheel for a while, and I was extremely thankful for that.

I spent early 2011 trying hard to remain sober. I looked fine, I acted fine, I functioned fine, but I was lost. I was wearing so many masks, I didn't know which one fitted the real me anymore. The parts I had been proud of had really started to crack and little bits of me just kept falling off everywhere every day. I began to think I was just a bad person, and that I didn't deserve to have anyone love me. There wasn't one bit of me that I liked anymore. I lived constantly in a world of shame and self-loathing. This was getting to be a rock bottom life, although I was to discover that rock bottom has many basements.

The marriage ended without much fanfare on my birthday in 2011. *He* got on a plane and returned home from a business trip in Queenstown when *he* heard from one of our staff that I'd turned up to our company with the smell of alcohol on my breath. I was escorted home. *He* turned up not much later; I couldn't work out how he got from Queenstown to Wellington so fast. I don't even remember us discussing the end, but it <u>was</u> the end and that part of my life with *him* was done.

Karen arrived that day also. She had planned to surprise me, but in return, she got caught up in the dirty water of *him* and me. I just wanted her to go home, but she has an excellent ability to stick like glue to me when all is coming unstuck. She stayed around for a few days to be with me and try and help me. All I could think of was that I now had the chance to freely drink out in the open again, and drink I did.

I went down the road to the local hairdresser's and had all my hair cut off. I've been blessed with massive amounts of hair, long, thick, and curly. You could say it was my crowning glory and one of the few things I liked about my appearance. The hairdresser refused to cut it to begin with, until I told her one of my many lies that I wanted to donate it to the people who make wigs for those who had lost their hair. I kept the hair myself for a few weeks looking at what I had done, until I couldn't anymore. I finally sent it off to the right organization. In a cruel twist, three years later I had all but lost all my hair to malnutrition.

I can't say I was sad that the marriage was over because I wasn't. I think by then I was just empty, and any desire to save things had disappeared a long time ago. I truly deeply loved *him* once, but I lived with always knowing I was second best. I chose to enter the relationship knowing that, but maybe I secretly hoped it would change in time to favor me just a little bit more. It didn't.

Our marriage withstood so many tests. Some we handled well… others not so well. My growing issues with the bottle and alcoholism are what I own. I hurt those I loved the most and will forever wish that it were different. I broke and I didn't know why, and I didn't know how to "fix it."

Since those days, I have stood witness to women and men like me who battled alcoholism and drug addiction along with other issues that led them on that path. A good percentage didn't make it to the other side, but oh my, those who did showed me that deep love and commitment can eventually conquer all.

*Susan and Blair, Antionette, and Jesse, the four
of you are such a beautiful shining example of
that and I love hanging around the glow of it.*

I felt extremely bad and sad for our youngest Jackson, but I had the idea that he would just continue to live with me, and maybe see more of his father now that there would be dedicated days and weekends set for them to spend together. It didn't happen like that.

I was moved out and into an area of Wellington that I was so uncomfortable with. My good friend, Barbs, told me at the time, "Get rid of your fancy clothes and, for God's sake, wear your pajama pants to the supermarket", "you stand out around here and that's not good." Thankfully, I was eventually given our dog Jesse, and so I was able to feel a little more secure. At the time, it's what I felt I deserved; a shit person living in a shit hole. I drank myself to stupidity, lived on two-minute noodles, placed stupid phone calls, and caused everyone who I loved to worry themselves silly over me.

The reality of Jackson not living with me, in a nice house, in a quaint area of Wellington was tough to bear. Soon after I was moved out of our house, *he* left for a planned trip with Jackson to Australia. Before departure, *he* informed me the locks had all been changed, and if I thought about going back to my home, the neighbors were told to call the police.

So, it started to become clear that this was how things were going to play out for now. I didn't fight; I didn't feel I had a right to anything, let alone my home and our son. I lasted about a month in that place until Karen phoned and said she had booked a ticket home to Queenstown for me. That was to signal the end of my time in Wellington for the time being. I packed up my sorry self, and I went home.

The first few days back home in Queenstown at Karen's house was nothing short of freaking hell. I didn't know back then that stopping alcohol just like that was dangerous. I'd called the Alcohol Helpline a few times before (quite a few times when I think back), and the advice I would often get and what I always clearly remembered was not to stop. They warned me that it was dangerous and could put your health at great risk. I heard that loud and clear.

I stopped plenty of times for days, weeks, and months on end, but I never felt like I was going to die the way I did those first few days back home. I didn't say anything; again, I felt it was my punishment for the weakness of continuing to pour alcohol down my gullet. So, I just internally and externally shook my way through the first days of withdrawal. It wasn't my first rodeo, and it wasn't going to be my last.

As I share this difficult time with you, I can feel the lasting effects of the pain. I shudder to write about those sixteen years, especially the last three to four years of a draining slow decline. As I am writing this, I have to stop frequently to escape the weight. I got up, I went to the beach, watched Netflix, did yoga, went to the pool to swim meditating lengths, called friends, talked the baby talk with my newborn grandson, and then came back to face the screen again. It's still draining me, and I am anxious to get to the good bits. Believe me, they are coming, but I had to pass through hell before I found my way back.

I needed to bring up the tragic part of my life again to be clear that I am not trying to deflect my actions on anyone. If I could have left *him* out, I would have. *He* exists there in those years, and I couldn't complete my story without mentioning *him*.

I stopped drinking with the resolve that this time I was really going to do it. I moved into Nellie's then-vacant home with another friend Justin, and I slowly morphed into a health nut. I walked about four kilometers each way, sometimes in the snow in the early, dark hours of the morning to go to the pool. I'd stay in the water forever swimming length after length, slowly shedding the heavy feeling that I was constantly carrying inside and out. When I'd start to feel lighter, and start to notice the sunshine, I'd get out and then go to the walking/rowing machines and use them to squeeze the self-loathing out of my head. By the time I'd thrown a Pilates class in and walked back home, I'd collapse.

I started to outwardly look fit and healthy, but the light was gone out in my eyes, and those who knew me best could see it. I tried antidepressants for about two minutes, but quickly realized that the "feel good" I was experimenting with the pool got sucked out with the effects of a pill. Plus, I hate drugs of any sort. After all, alcohol is one. Right? I walked around Queenstown with my head down. I didn't want to see people who knew me and tried to lie my way around where Jackson was and why I was back.

About six weeks after I arrived home, *he* flew down with Jackson. Seeing my darling twelve-year-old helped fill up my mother's heart.

The purpose of the visit was to have me removed off a couple of trusts, business documents, and everything that we had built over the last numerous years. Short of signing divorce papers and deciding on a settlement, the marriage partnership on paper was quickly dissolved. He had asked Nelly to be present, so she was there to have the joy of hearing this.

On putting the pen down after completing all the paperwork that I didn't give a shit about, he looked at me and said, "I'll always love you. Then he called me by *his* late wife's name. That summed up my life with *him.*

Nelly said afterward that she wouldn't blame me if I had a drink after that experience. I didn't. I waited until it was confirmed to me a couple of weeks later that *he* was in a relationship with the chick who lived across the road from our house in Wellington, and then I let loose like there was no tomorrow. If my drinking was looking shaky before, it would have nothing on what I did next.

We were divorced inside a year, and they were engaged not long after. *He* legally kept custody of Jackson who was to continue school in the Lower Hutt area and go onto boarding school as we had always planned. After raising five children, we were one year short of being semi-childless part-time at home during the week at least. I was on my way to "drunk" Denise when I appeared for that divorce/custody hearing, and all I really heard the judge say was the word "alcoholic" again and again.

I may sound bitter, but I'm not. I'm only writing the facts. "Alcoholic" was fast becoming a well-used label that I was now known by. There was no holding back on that. I didn't want it, I didn't seek to be one, and it was not the path I dreamed my life would take, but that was what I'd become.

I always felt that I was clearly second best, and that's all there was to it. I understood it when I met *him*, I accepted it, and I lived with it. Hell, at times I even embraced it. I allow myself to wander here and now while I'm ending the story of *him*, and as I am letting *him* float away out of my head and life again.

> *Would it have been different, if just once you'd*
> *made me feel like I was first, that I really mattered*
> *most in your world now, and if you had gathered*
> *me tightly into your arms often enough and told*
> *me so, would the ending have been different?*

# CHAPTER 11

# *Relapse*

Picking up the bottle and entering active drunkenness again was hard work. Very quickly, my cognitive thinking became soaked in alcohol. Blackouts were becoming more and more frequent. They had started the year before, but the intensity that they were reaching was frightening.

I was apparently making a lot of phone calls to friends, calls that I didn't remember the next morning. I was constantly crying over the phone, very much feeling sorry for myself, which wasn't in my character, and I was beginning to quickly piss off all those close to me. Almost all of this was done in a complete blackout. I looked like I was functioning and sounded normal… until I didn't.

I later read a book about a woman who had spent her entire thirties in blackout from alcohol. I could relate to everything she wrote. I was about to spend the best part of the next three years of my life just like that. The clouds of darkness had descended on me. There were pieces of those three years that I want to say I felt some warmth. But they are all in a mixing bowl combined with bad places I was going to, bad things that I was doing, and the bad person I felt I'd become.

Nelly and Karen gave it another good shot to get me to see a mental health worker in Queenstown. She was a local like me, and we had a history because we went to school together. She knew my history, who I was, who I had married, my children, my job—all of it. None of that should have mattered, but it did to me. I was fast becoming the shadow of a person I used to be proud of; admitting that to myself was hard enough. I certainly didn't want to admit it to someone I knew.

She did her job with compassion plus some, and arranged for me to go across the Road to the Lakes District hospital for medical detox. That was no easy feat, but believe me, today it is almost unheard of. DHBs don't have Detox beds; the government took care of that.

Did I have hope that this would help me? No. I didn't want it. I wanted to live in the nightmare I'd created for myself. Other people's need for me to be sober wasn't enough, and I didn't like 'me' sober. I didn't want reality. I only wanted numbness.

The staff during that detox was incredible. The kindness they showed me was unique. One nurse had been where I was, so she tried to help me get on a decent path to find  support by taking me to some AA meetings. Five years later, I was able to repay the kindness she showed me when she admitted herself to the private rehab where I was employed. I have heard from her in recent times, so I know she is living her best life now.

Blackouts pretty much occurred after I left the hospital. One of the last memories I have, before I was discharged, was Toni Okkerse coming to my room. Toni was my nurse when I delivered Joel; she later became my neighbor for ten years, with my son playing big brother to her two young children. She is an angel on earth that all who know her will confirm. She doesn't need words; her presence brings you an instant feeling of calm, while always carrying a glow of kindness around her.

One day, Toni told me my parents were in the visitor's room. How they even found Toni to tell her they were there; I still don't know. I was shocked that they wanted to drive over from their home in Alex to see me. I know I embarrassed them greatly, so I didn't expect the reception I received when I entered the room. They had flowers that Mum had picked from her garden; the sight of those broke me. They loved me and they were there for me, and it should have been enough to turn me, but it wasn't.

Any acts of kindness just added to the book of total shame and disgust that was now occupying a massive part of my thoughts.

The length my parents went to try and get me help was proof that the love of a child remains unconditional. Parents whose children are addicts reach a point that they realize they just can't afford to continue to love them to death. Their unconditional love never faded, but the conditions by which they chose to stand by and watch helplessly as their daughter destroyed herself eventually had to be enforced. They, too, had to stand momentarily in the shadows, waiting and wishing I'd come to my senses and stop.

One clear memory I had before the next bender boomed into total blackout chaos was my mother talking on the phone to an old support worker that I'd had in Wellington. I'd somehow ended up at my parent's house through my father all but dragging me over there. I know I fought him, memory scar # 1001.

My mother got off the phone, and at 8 am, drove down to the supermarket to purchase two bottles of wine. She was advised to slowly detox me with small amounts of wine. Good advice that I've used hundreds of times since. I was so grateful for the reprieve from withdrawal, but there was no end game to this by then. I didn't have help to go to, and even if there was, I didn't want it. What it did was unleash the warrior in me that alcohol fed, and I fled. I fled via spilling a tale to Nelly who had a pub nearby, and from there I hitchhiked home in the early hours of the morning to Queenstown.

Running became the answer. If I hung around Queenstown too long, I feared that someone, somehow, would try and take my Sav away from me again. It had been happening for so long—friends searching the house for bottles I'd hidden, going as far as to take my money cards, my cash, even my phone sometimes, so I couldn't call a cab and get to a bank to get money to get to the supermarket to get wine to get to a place in my head that I could forget, to get numb, and to stay dead inside.

So that's what I did. I kept running. I'm not proud of any of it, I used and abused anyone who showed weakness and kindness to me. The many masks I wore hid the fact that my only concern and needs were to be somewhere safe so I could consume my savior.

I made it to Wanaka, and when I became too much there, I used another person to get me to Christchurch and the safety of his home for a time. I didn't intentionally prey on kind people. I was respectful, and I wore the right mask for the right person in that right situation of the time, but there's no denying I used people to be in a safe place to safely stay in a blackout. I haven't seen or spoken to that person who drove in the snow from Christchurch to Wanaka and back to help me since 2011.

*I hope life has been kind to you as you were to me,*
*and I'm deeply sorry I made you part of my mess.*

The memory box of shameful scars grew from there. There are so many; shame was my second name. I used those memory scars in the early days and months of life over the bottle. I used the wounds that I had created for myself and for what I had done to others to become my wings. I used them to remind myself of where I had come, and as fuel to get me to where I was heading.

From 2014 on, I made amends with words, and even more in actions. I waited and I believed that in time, those who loved me, and those who mattered, would find forgiveness for what I'd become. I waited for time, love, and courage to heal.

If I were to paint a picture of what my world looked like at this point, my life on canvas was like a paint shop that had exploded. Mostly the red, blue, and black colors like the angry bruises my body was constantly producing. I taught my half-dead well mind to drop and roll when I reached the almost pass-out level. Falling over and hurting myself was a regular dance step I'd acquired. I'd crawl to bed when the darkness was coming, and I'd crawl out when I'd wake up and need to seek it all over again.

Something deep inside me wanted to survive, and my half-dead well mind would surface now and again, just in time to save me more times than I'd like to remember.

C H A P T E R  12

# *The last train stop.*

In September 2011, I had a phone call from my father. In my world, when Dad wants to talk to me, it means serious business. My parents had stood back from trying to force, beg, and persuade me to stop, so it was a surprise that they even found me. My phone was permanently turned off, or possibly disconnected, I can't remember… blackout blank. Still, they found me.

My father used these words.

> *Denise, it would mean every birthday,*
> *Father's Day, and Christmas rolled into one*
> *if you would just do this one thing for me.*
> *Appear in court tomorrow and say yes to*
> *going to a place that's going to help you.*

Unbeknownst to me at the time, and until some years later, it had already been arranged that I was going to a little farm, whether I liked it or not. Taking myself to court was one step away from being forced to court, so my parents wanted to try and give me the chance to say yes I wanted it, rather than them saying, 'You're going no matter what.'

So, I did. Dad's asking was enough to awaken my life-long need to please other people, especially someone I loved so dearly. If I could do this to make him and my mother feel a little better, I thought, 'Why not?' A reprieve and just maybe, possibly someone or something could help me feel some hope again, so it was worth a try.

I truly thought a place on a farm in the country where I could help with their commercial garden, where I would receive counseling, have group therapy, and be cared for was going to be a turning point. I deeply, truly felt a shimmer of hope for the first time in forever.

Firstly, I had to get blind drunk, go out with a bang, the last party, blah… blah. Everyone does it; believe me. In the later years when I worked in rehab, I only ever had two people out of over hundreds arrive sober for admission.

The Christchurch earthquake in February 2011 happened seven months before I went to court, so a lot of major buildings and government departments had moved out of the central city. I turned up to court very obviously the worse for wear with no actual clear idea of why I was standing in a courtroom on an airbase. That I was at an airbase registered, even making me think, oh goodie, maybe I'm being flown somewhere warm.

I don't know most of what the judge said. I didn't even see the judge through Sav-fogged eyes. Somewhere in those minutes, I must have said yes to the rehab plan. I don't know who was with me, and I didn't know what much of it meant, but the next minute I was being led out and taken in a car. Destination: hospital.

The Kennedy detox center on the same grounds as Hillmorton Hospital in Christchurch was and still is an amazing caring place. The staff were professional and compassionate and knew what they were doing when it came to medically detoxing people off drugs and alcohol.

If only New Zealand had 100 more Kennedys attached to psychology-based rehabs. If only…

The first indication I had that all was not chipper was when I couldn't walk out the door and have a cigarette. The doors were kept locked. It registered with me then that maybe I didn't want to do this after all. Over the next few days, I was heavily sedated with Diazepam, which I'd come to bloody hate. They were required. I know this now, but feeling drugged wasn't the way I rolled. I always seemed to have control over the slow or fast way I could medicate myself on alcohol. Benzos like Diazepam were different. They hung around, and they made me sluggish and sad.

The next clear thing I remember was someone, either another patient or nurse, telling me that I couldn't leave and go anywhere on my own. Fair enough—I was only halfway through detox. But then it started to sink in: there were rules around me. It took 14 days at Kennedy for me to recover to a semi-safe health presentation along with regaining clarity. For a good many of those days, I was progressing enough to get thick needles full of complex Vitamin B1 jabbed into my bum.

Thiamine is one of the B family's most important brain juices and one that those who suffer from alcoholism are mostly always depleted of. It is medically established that those suffering severe deficiency in Thiamine directly create a condition called Wernicke-Korsakoff syndrome (WKS). Other symptoms from Thiamine deficiency can be contributed to significant forms of alcohol-induced brain injury, and varying degrees of cognitive impairment. Not being able to walk unaided or using a walker, a 40-year-old person could look and sound like they were 90.

Wet brain, as it's commonly called, is simply horrible. And it's common and extremely hard to recover from. It's like you've had a stroke; I've seen many cases of WKS, more than I'd care to remember. Mostly from the insides of rehabs, none more than from where I was about to head.

I've diverted for a minute and slipped into my world of today. Please take note of what I've written if you or someone you're watching over is consuming large amounts of alcohol, and if you do nothing other than this, take yourself or them to your doctor and get prescribed Thiamine. It might just save you from becoming trapped within forever with no chance of ever escaping the effects of this disease. I have often asked a doctor who is examining a client of mine to add this to the list of medications. I've sat and watched some doctors look up the facts around it in astonishment as they took out their prescription pads.

I <u>love</u> it when I meet doctors who state that they will administer an injection of Thiamine to someone who is clearly on the dark side of alcohol, or ones who suggest it before I do and say they will add the B screening to the blood tests. It happened recently here in Thailand with a young female doctor who was presented with my client who wanted to detox off a recent short but hard relapse.

Back to Kennedy—around day ten to fourteen, it was explained to me that I had voluntarily put myself under section 8 of the Alcoholism and Drug act of 1966 while trying to stand up straight in court that day. Not to be confused with the Mental Health Act; that didn't hold as much punch as the AOD Act did. Pretty fucked up really.

I no longer had any choices. I was going to a place that I couldn't leave until a CEO, a judge, and a court said I could. For the next two years, if I was found consuming alcohol, I'd be brought right back. If I were found purchasing alcohol or in a place that served alcohol, I could be detained and all rights of freedom revoked, and I would be brought right back. That little farm homestay rehab wasn't looking so hopeful after all.

If you think that's all a bit far-fetched for New Zealand in 2011, it wasn't. I tested it, and I learned in just two horrifying days after a well-fought month's fight for freedom that it's bloody well real.

# CHAPTER 13

## *It's all over rova at Nova.*

One of the first things I was made aware of when I arrived at Nova was that, although the government subsidizes a patient's stay there, the patient is also made to pay for it ultimately. I was promptly taken to a doctor down the road who spent seconds with me, then wrote a medical certificate for the then-sickness benefit.

That money went directly to the Nova coffers and I was given $47 weekly. It was the same for everyone. All meals were free, but patients paid for everything else, such as coffee and any sugar treats that every person craved. Coffee and sugar are standard cravings after ceasing most substances.

I had my own money, unlike 80% of people there. I could afford cigarettes, which were also high on the list of needs. Most couldn't, so it wasn't uncommon for people to beg and borrow or to go around the trash cans and collect used tobacco butts.

Every Friday, we went as a group to the supermarket for about 90 minutes, and after five weeks onsite, we were able to go out on weekend days alone.

The crowning glory of Nova's policies was that patients were able to drink alcohol and use drugs. The punishment for getting caught was a five-week stand down from the privilege of going out into the real world unsupervised. Any other sane rehab that I knew of before and every single one I dealt with since either stands patients down for several days, sometimes allowing them to return, or directly discharges them. The fact that no one had any money to go out anyway meant that taking away that privilege meant sweet nothing.

There was another way out: if patients were caught sleeping with someone in either the male or female wings, they were instantly discharged. Like how fucked up is that. It was a so-called rehab where people could get away with drinking and drugging, yet if they slept with someone, they were out. Nova in my mind had a very confused sense of what it was actually intended to be.

The CEO, Joy, on several occasions, would all but proudly state that the facility had about a two percent success rate and that they were a revolving door. In truth, it was a door that was spinning around, subsidized by the government therefore costing the taxpayer about $900 per person per week, plus the sickness benefit they had us all on. On top of that, we worked for no wages, so effectively there was truly little outgoing and a huge amount of money incoming. It amused me on trustee meeting nights watching the latest models of flashy cars cruise up the long and winding driveway.

There was an average of 60 "inmates" (our name for each other) on a property that spanned 80 acres. What we didn't want to have happen was our alcohol or our drug stash being found. Given that there were 80 acres to hide it in, chances were slim that it would be. There was a pub called the golden mile that was a good, golden few kilometers or so to run at the end of a long road. With only one supervisor every evening from 4 pm to 7 am, there were a lot of very fit people who could get down there and back unnoticed daily. So almost everyone drank. I didn't—not there anyway. I don't know why, it just wasn't my MO to drink under lock and key.

Some couldn't afford alcohol and resorted to other methods like methylated spirits. It's cheaper and they have the same kinds of effects they get from the alcohol fast. Perfume or hand sanitizer was a close second, but that was even nastier than the purple poison. Watching people pursue these alternative methods goes down as one of the most horrible events I witnessed at that hell hole. One girl was prone to drinking this poison all the time, but one time she overdid it. She was in agonizing pain, vomiting, and defecating everywhere. A girl in my wing was a nurse. Catherine decided to go down and let the staff know. It meant a stand down again for the poor woman, but her condition now called for serious medical attention, if not an ambulance fast.

Staffing was minimal in Nova; everything was run by the inmates. However, they did have a community nurse from Monday to Friday. We called her Panadol Vicki because that drug was her answer to everything. Her diagnosis of what was wrong with a patient was woeful. Believe me, even if people were almost dying, they rarely got to see a doctor—let alone a hospital.

Panadol and an upgrade to the sickbay was all this poor girl received, accompanied by two of us who rotated with two others for around 48 hours to try and help her get through the excruciating pain she was in. We spent those days cleaning her up, caring for her, and doing our best to offer her what comfort we could while Panadol Vicki just went home.

The next time this happened, Catherine just took matters into her own hands and surprised the hell out of Panadol Vicki by calling an ambulance. The look of shock on her face when the ambulance turned up was priceless.

We had a gentle elderly lady come into Nova whom we all treated with much respect; some saw her as a grandmother. No one would swear around her, and all went out of their way to help and watch over her. After hurting her leg walking into some furniture, she sought some help from Panadol Vicki, and yes, she was given Panadol. Over the coming days, we could tell her leg was causing her great pain. She was unable to walk, so we started taking her meals to her. Caring Catherine once again went to Nova's poor excuse for a nurse and insisted that further medical attention was required. Panadol Vicki's answer to this was that the old woman was seeking attention, and we should stop taking her meals to her.

Of course, nothing was done. By day five, Catherine called the ambulance once again herself. We didn't see our lovely surrogate grandmother for another three weeks. She stayed in the care and professional company of Christchurch Hospital orthopedic ward while the two broken bones she suffered in her leg had a chance to start to mend.

I don't care about slandering Panadol Vicki. I could dedicate an entire chapter to the disgusting lack of care and compassion she showed the people of Nova. No sickness or injury went any further than her unless the person wanted to risk the loss of privilege by going over her head to the CEO or directly calling 111emergency services. I watched so many people suffer so unnecessarily because of her. I believe in Karma, and I hope to this day that what went around came around for her.

This was a government-subsidized, non-government organization (NGO) that had zero professional care. The so-called counselors were all first and second-year students doing their degrees in substance abuse. Some tried to make a difference but were ill-equipped to do so professionally. I felt they did more damage than good. Many of us came back from our weekly or fortnightly sessions more messed up than what we already were going into them. As for me, I just gave up on them altogether after a while. I sat in my therapy sessions and watched paint dry while white noise happened around me.

Group sessions involved reading literature out of a textbook. AA groups were held every Friday on the premises just amongst the residents for about 20 minutes, then we would sit there for the rest of the required hour watching the world pass us by. Nobody was willing to speak up within a group of people they lived with every minute of the day. Now and again, someone from the outside world would appear, and we'd all sit a little straighter out of respect and anticipation that we might hear a message of hope. One man who came every week loved to add another number to his growing count of people he knew who had died due to addiction. That's the reason I refuse to count all those lost souls who didn't make it.

As I said, we ran the place. The kitchen had two chefs, one full-time and one part-time. We did all the rest. Feeding 70-odd people including the staff was a big job. We grew baby beets, cucumbers, and capsicums. The garden was a separate business from Nova itself. We all had jobs, so people either worked the greenhouses, the kitchen, the cleaning, or whatever else was needed to house and manage so many people.

I'd moved inside from working in the greenhouses once they figured out I could cook. My ability to create appetizing, large quantities of decent food presented itself when a sudden heavy snowstorm hit us. Our guess was the management of the profit-making produce operation knew the storm was on its way. The first signs to alert us that something was up was when the temperature dropped rapidly in our wings and in the main buildings, and the heat from the boilers was redirected away from us and into the tunnel houses.

The next sign came when all the staff packed up and left for home, not returning for three days. The residents settled in for three joyful days without them while the snow dumped down. Two other women helped me cook up another storm by using everything we liked to eat from cold storage that was meant for a month. The staff eventually returned when the snow started to clear, not that we really cared. They worked in their areas, and we existed in ours.

I felt sorry for the chef as she had to account for all that budgeted food that we used to fill our bellies. She was a happy soul who made the job of kitchen helper one that was highly sought after.

She was late turning up to work one morning, so I went down to the offices to collect the keys and open the fridges and dry stock. Nothing was shocking or touching my emotions at that point, but when I was told by the office staff that I needed to take over for the day in the kitchen because our chef had died in her sleep the night before, I was floored. She was young, she was healthy as far as we knew, she had a loving husband and young children, and she just died. We asked to go to her funeral service, those few of us who had worked closely with her day in and day out, but we were denied that privilege. Like all other decisions, no reason was given.

There were so many unwell people living in Nova over the time I spent there. All of us arrived in different stages of disrepair, damage, and shock. We came from all over the country, arriving after we had detoxed. Some knew they were destined for Nova, having committed themselves under section 8 of the Act voluntarily like I unknowingly had. Then there were the ones who arrived under section 9. They were on a different level to begin with, when they arrived. The "9s" normally had no idea what was coming to them. I felt so sorry for them when I first arrived in Nova and watched them enter. As time passed, I stopped caring as much for them as I slowly started caring less and less about everyone and everything around me.

A '9' had to have a family member, a doctor, and a judge sign an order for them to be extracted from their place of residence, placed on a plane, and accompanied to Christchurch. Often, this was done with the police taking part in the entire operation, and often it was without any warning to the soon-to-be inmate. A person could be happily sitting at home thinking everything was as normal as an addict's normal could be. The next minute, they could be beamed to Christchurch City.

Christchurch suffered a tragic earthquake on February 22nd, 2011, so aftershocks were common, and often about half a dozen a day. So, for a person who had never experienced that, it was shocking to suddenly live in a place where the ground was rocking and rolling beneath your feet numerous times of the day and night.

Not only did these people suffer the shock and trauma of the events that had suddenly happened in their lives, but they also had to quickly adapt to the earthquakes. Some aftershocks were just enough to lift your drink up. Others required us to quickly move outside. The nasty part was that we just didn't know what was happening until it was upon us. I think the sound of the rumble that came before the quake messed with our heads as much as the constant quakes themselves. It was worse when they occurred in the night after I'd finally fallen asleep. To wake up with a jolt was nerve-wracking. Just like everything, good or bad, the longer you're in it, the more it just becomes the norm. That said, I still sleep with everything I need in case of emergency, packed and by my bed at night all these years later.

So, there I was in 2011 at 46 years old, a woman who had come from so much to this awful excuse for a rehab facility. It was the last train stop for alcoholics. Still, no one had ever sat down and asked me why I turned to alcohol, no one heard me, and no one diagnosed me. I had been given a label, and it stuck. This was me. Denise the alcoholic, living in a place where alcoholics go directed by the court.

I had a drunk driving charge that I wasn't proud of in the slightest, and I had a speeding ticket. That was my rap sheet.

I was stuck, so I gave up, and I sank. I pretended to everyone around me that life was ok. I conformed to everything that was required of me. I naturally started thinking and speaking in self-deprecating terms. I learned to say, "Can I please," or "Is it ok if," for every movement and action I was making. Everything had to be cleared whether it was a trip to the shop or an outing like a weekend day trip. It was boarding school on a whole other ugly level.

Due to the way I presented, I was repeatedly asked to be the person who accompanied a male staff member to do roundups. This meant going with him to houses, hospitals, and wherever else someone had run off to, to collect and bring back the escapees. This could play out with them screaming and fighting it, or it could play out arguing with gang members at the house where they were hiding who did not want to let them go. I was just cold, and I didn't care. These missions represented time out of that awful place, and that seemed enough for me. The next step up in bringing people back was an escort courtesy of the police, but normally they had to have committed a crime to get a ride back that way.

I became institutionalized quickly. I lived with so little self-worth that I felt this was what I deserved. I said for years after that place, "Nova stole my soul". I didn't drink there, but I looked forward to the day when I could again. I sat and waited for the day when the CEO decided I could leave. I never had a hint when those days were coming. 3 months or 6 months, it was at her discretion. When she felt I was ready, I would be released. How she could tell me my level of readiness, I have no idea. It certainly couldn't have come from the reports from my so-called 'counselor' as I'd learned to tell her nothing.

Everyone lived in a state of anxiety as to when they could get out and go home. Some didn't have a home anymore. Some wanted to be there. Some had just given up all hope of having a chance to change. Some stayed there long past their time waiting to die.

The first thing I did when I was let out in January 2012 was to go and drink. No second thought to it whatsoever. No second thought to anyone but me and my need to find numbness.

My parents had given me their second car, so I drove it somewhere I could drink. The rest was a blackout. A woman I met in Nova agreed to drive with me back to Wellington. She drove, and I drank. The whole trip was in a blackout.

Deep down, I still believed I could make something decent out of myself despite my desperate circumstances. My past was proof of that. So, while at Nova, I applied to do a health science course in Wellington. I had to jump through some hoops and be present in online interviews. With no formal education behind me after leaving school before my High School exams, I was shocked when I was accepted. The plan was to follow the dream I had from a really young age and become a nurse. I really don't remember much of my childhood, but it was always with me that this is what I wanted to become.

That opportunity went downhill as quickly as the wine went down my throat. I had a house I had rented in Wellington. I had no furniture but that was to be arranged. I remember spending about five minutes at that house, myself, and this woman, before deciding to continue up the road to Palmerston North. There was another woman we called Maid Marion, who lived there, and so on we went to crash her reestablished life.

To conclude my short-lived freedom from Nova, it all ended via a ride in an ambulance, a barefooted escape from the hospital, another drunk driving charge, and me in blackout apparently saying I didn't want to live and begging Nova to take me back.

When I woke up, I found myself in Kennedy, Christchurch again, wondering what just happened. I went from freedom from Nova to imprisonment to the bottle within hours and really had no memory of any of it. That's how quickly things can turn from good to ugly once alcoholism owns you.

"Rock bottoms with basements became
a solid foundation on which I later
used to rebuild my life" – *Denise*

# CHAPTER 14

# *Next stop, basement*

I repeat, hell has basements. If I thought I was soulless before, I was about to learn what it felt like to lose more of me. Once back in Nova, I quickly took up the position of Queen Bee, something I'd never done in my life before. A lovely woman called Linda had arrived and taken over my room while I was gone. Within 24 hours of returning, I had her out and I settled back into what was familiar to me. What made me, me, had all but gone. I was emotionally dead inside. I didn't blame others, I owned what I'd become, but I was now heading towards feeling nothingness.

My children were all that kept my head just above the surface. They were my heartbeat, and they were the reason that a tiny sliver of me would hold some hope that I could eventually overcome this, that I could control alcohol rather than letting it control me.

When I talked to my children, I lied about events to try and protect the ugliness of what their mother had become. I told them everything was fine. I told them I just felt I needed more time back at Nova, blah, blah, lie, lie.

Later, I found my voice and was able to express the effect that being placed under the act had on me. I was asked to be part of a study around a draft in place to reform and change the outdated AOD Act of 1966. As with anything that involves a government when it comes to addiction, it was to be a long road with the changes to the old Act not coming into play in 2018—six years later.

Nova came into my life because my family and two close friends were informed that it offered a place for me to get help. They were living a life of hell because of my addiction. My mother not sleeping at night. She reached a point of such resignation that she had started planning my funeral in her head. The original mental health worker from Queenstown who was advising my parents, sister, and Nelly and Karen felt that Nova was a good option but had never been there to actually observe how it operated.

Patients can only enter Nova if they are under either Section 8 (voluntary) or Section 9 (compulsory) of the AOD 1966 Act. I presume this is how Nova was able to gain the financial subsidies from the Government.

The professional help that was promised on their website and presented on paper did not exist within its 80 acres. I'm sure they had policies that had to be written in reports and on brochures, but the reality was nothing close to the propaganda.

If people wanted any real professional help, they had to fight for it. Often it was an outside family member or professional body who was able to help people get referred to outside professional services. Some but very few with comorbid conditions such as eating disorders and diagnosed mental health issues were lucky enough to receive the care they deserved. Most weren't. Any attempt of suggestions of change and for further professional help for addiction were met with a firm 'NO.' It's not how things were done, and raising a fuss about it got people tagged as troublemakers. It was the perfect prison.

Mental health had no word association at all to addiction. We were Alcoholics and Drug Addicts. As the wording in the Alcoholism and Drug Addiction act of 1966 dictated, I was there due to Alcoholism.

The act of 1966 stated:

> Alcoholic/Drug Addict means a person
> whose persistent and excessive indulgence in
> alcohol/ drugs is causing or is likely to cause
> serious injury to his health or is a source
> of harm, suffering, or serious annoyance
> to others or renders him incapable of
> properly managing himself or his affairs.

It's now been upgraded to the Substance Addiction (Compulsory Assessment and Treatment) Act of 2017 that finally came into effect in 2018.

If you were to google the Act now, you will see that it's become a lot more politically correct than its predecessor. Among other things, it outlines the following:

> That the intention is to protect them from
> serious harm, stabilize their health, protect, and
> enhance their mana and dignity, and restore
> their capacity to make informed decisions
> about further treatment for substance use.

Under the act that is in effect now, it is a lot harder to have someone assessed and placed. I know this as I've been part of a family's process to try and have their daughter placed under the act. Their daughter had been placed into good professional treatment clinics, and some not so good places like Nova, around 15 in total as I recall.

She was living on the streets and in and out of the hospital for injuries sustained while consistently being drunk or in a blackout. She was suffering daily head injuries from falling, the ambulances refused to pick her up, the hospitals were finding ways of not admitting her, and the police were trying to leave her at my house once they found my services. I'll never forget them standing at my gated apartment block and telling me that she was harmless. They insisted that I had a social obligation to take her, as I watched her climb over from the back seat and throw the police car in reverse in an attempt to escape.

Nothing was stopping her, so the family tried to reinforce what they knew from the old AOD act and have her admitted into a Salvation Army bridge program that would at least keep her safe. The doctor had second thoughts, refuted her statement, and that was the end of that. I disengaged soon after. I hope she survived and found she was worthy of a good life.

# CHAPTER 15

# *The great escape*

A few months after I returned to my nightmare of life in Nova, I travelled up to Wellington to take care of my quickie divorce. Normally when I went home, I didn't drink. This time it was a weekday break out of Nova due to the court hearing, therefore I didn't get to see my young son at boarding school. So, combined with the emotion surrounding the court hearing and time out on my own, I did what I did best to deal with difficult emotional events, and I drank—lots.

Timing when to stop was a big thing. If I returned to Nova with an alcohol reading, I'd be stood down for five weeks and unable to travel north again to see my youngest son. These trips were what kept me partly together, spending time with him. It was easy to forget what I'd become while being able to be a present mother again.

Unbeknownst to Nova, on one of my trips to Wellington, I secured a place in a house with a couple of firemen. They were always on shift work and came and went at different times, so my spin to them that I worked on the road in the film industry was an easy lie to cover my long absences. Absolutely no one knew of my rental house except for Barb.

Nova had an address for Barb, my roomie from the Lower Hutt rehab days, and that's where they thought I was staying. They had done their job, which surprised me, and called ahead to make sure I was staying with her and to alert her of my status under the act. Of course, I wasn't staying with her. I was parked up in my nice house in the burbs in Wellington.

At 2 am before I flew back to Christchurch, I stopped drinking, but that was five hours later than I should have, to allow for the alcohol to reach undetectable levels. We were all smart about the timeframes when the alcohol would be out of our systems enough not to read on a breathalyzer, and I was sailing close to the edge on this one. I forced down bottles of water together with other tricks I had learned until I was confident that, when I arrived back, I'd be in the clear.

Normally, I'd swan around before being stopped, and another hour or so would pass before they realized I needed to be tested. This time, Panadol Vicki was all but waiting for me at the front gate. They knew I had gone home for a court hearing and the finalization of my marriage, so odds were high that I may have consumed alcohol due to the stress and trauma of the visit.

I blew 80 on the breathalyzer. (If you cleanse your mouth with Listerine that has alcohol in it, you'll register around 80.) I was caught. I'd had a party with my best friend Sav, and I was now about to pay a big price for it. I could live with that if it weren't for my son. Five weeks would go by until I saw him again.

I lived under the government rules in an establishment that punished people who did the very thing they were addicted to. It made no sense. Still, I knew the rules, and I'd royally fucked up with not being clever enough to stop in time. Excuses were my surname. But getting a divorce along with being told—rightfully so—that *he* had custody of Jackson due to my alcoholism was right up there in my novel of excuses. Nova didn't see it like that, and I was slapped with a five-week stand down right there and then.

It had been a long time since I sought attention for the heart flutters I suffered. Years before, I'd been under a cardiologist who told me my heart murmur and prolapsed mitral value was controllable without drugs if I just found a way to be calm when the flutters happened. He had advised me to take lots of big breaths and apply icy cold water to my pulse points.

My heart rhythm dancing to a beat of great irregularity (arrhythmias) was a condition that I was used to, but when you throw a panic attack amongst this, it can become really scary. Although it's common for people who suffer from chronic panic attacks to feel like their hearts are going to jump out of their chests, I constantly get a double whammy when I start to feel trapped and stress closes in on me.

It felt like I'd become the latest greatest catch for Vicki and other management, Joy the CEO included. I broke in front of them all there and then. I really broke. I was sobbing uncontrollably, letting my emotions show for the first time ever in front of them. Of course, my episode was met with "You know the rules and now you'll pay for your actions."

As the realization set in, so did a horrible panic attack. I made it back to my wing where the women gathered around me thinking someone must have died. I couldn't breathe; the pain in my chest made me think I was really having a true heart attack. I was scared frozen.

This may all sound a little overdramatic for the events that had just occurred, but I held my emotions in for a long time. I never processed things the things that were happening to me. I'd just take this, and I'd take that, then I'd throw it all into a well inside me, firmly placing a lid on it. The lid had exploded off, and I didn't know which way was up.

Eventually, with the help of that small group of women I had allowed myself to become close to, I was able to calm down. Then reality sunk in. Was this my life, would I ever get out of here, would this be me forever, and most of all, what have I done to my youngest son, yet again?

That's when I decided:

*I'm done with you Nova, I'm running!*

# CHAPTER 16

# On the Run

It wasn't uncommon for people to run from Nova; it happened a lot. For some of us who didn't want to go down the path of purposely getting caught in bed with another person, running was the second and only other sure way you'd know what date you were going to depart this prison.

So, over the afternoon, together with the girls, I planned my great escape. I booked a flight back to Wellington. I had one of the girl's husbands arrange to meet me at the edge of the property. I would connect with him there at the perimeter after we had watched all the staff depart in their cars, making the meeting point safe from the chance of anyone from Nova driving by.

I'm an alcoholic, so Tony, who was meeting me, was directed to buy my supplies and have them ready for my arrival at freedom's door on the edge of that country road.

I gave all my clothes and possessions away. We sat in my room and figured out who was getting what. Linda was given the rights to my room again—best in the wing, of course. And I was set to take flight.

One of the girls went over to distract Kevin, who was the supervisor on duty that night, just in case he decided to wander the grounds around the time of my planned disappearance. Then, because it was getting dark and Lindy Loo made regular trips through the trees nightly to the golden mile bottle shop, she and I set off to find my rendezvous point. Through the trees, through the paddocks under the electric fences, and around the cows that ignored me, I made it to the gate, to the car, to my wine, to the airport, and to my freedom.

*Screw you, Nova, it's over and Im out!*

The last thing I did before I fell asleep in my bed in Wellington that night was to phone the supervisor, Kevin. He was a really nice man who was just trying to earn a living while studying to be a person who could make a difference in the lives of people like me. I'll never know if he ever became a counselor. I hope he did; he would have done that job well. I didn't want him to get into any serious trouble by not checking whether I was in my wing or not that night. So, I gave him the heads up I was now far, far away. I apologized that I ran on his shift, but he could at least file a report telling management that he had discovered I was missing before they worked it out who-knows-when over the next few days.

I'd watched enough great escapes to suspect that I should take my sim card out of my phone and get a new one so I couldn't be tracked. Then I worried that if something happened to the kids, they couldn't get hold of me. So, I got another cheap phone and would turn it off and on to check messages when I was out and away from the house. Barbs had my new number, and she would send me updates on any phone calls that came from Nova. Barbs was the only number and only address they had. I felt I was fairly safe in my little Wellington home.

As I said, if the history of others doing a "runner" was anything to go by, I presumed that after a week or so they would just give up and let me go. In the months I'd been in Nova, nobody who ran was ever brought back.

It didn't work like that for me. Joy had my number, and she wanted me back. To this day, I'll never know why. I was a model inmate up to the day I returned from the divorce hearing and blew the low reading. I'd never broken a rule. They used me for rounding up and cleaning up often—sometimes in the dead of night—going to collect some poor soul who had run only to find they had no place to go. If one of the girls either in my wing or one of the others was having a breakdown, I'd be called in to try and calm and reassure her. I'd sit for hours beside the bed of a girl who would be found in one of the paddocks so drunk that she had passed out. I watched over her all night to ensure she didn't choke on her vomit in her sleep.

I always worked the required 6-hour shift every day when the majority of inmates would just stay in their rooms and hide. Those who really suffered serious mental health issues were being dealt with by drugging them up to the eyeballs. Not me. I headed committees. I did what I was told while quietly seething with hatred for what this place was and what it was turning me into.

But none of that mattered. Joy was determined to hunt me down. And hunt me down, she did. My survival skills kicked in by doing things such as drawing out a large amount of cash, so I never had to use machines that would reveal my location. I laid low in the house most of the day, and, to my surprise, I completely backed up the bus with the amount I was drinking.

Around Easter, I decided to do a tiki tour to Nelson. It was only a ferry ride over the Cook Strait, and I knew a guy there who had spent forever coming and going from Nova. He was a nice man and a good friend. He was harmless, and I could trust him. So, off I went.

By this time, Joy had quit calling me, quit leaving messages, and had handed my case over to the police in Christchurch instead. I left my phone on while in Nelson, and decided to risk answering it to find out exactly how much trouble I was really in. The same cop who'd left all the prior messages left this one:

> *If you can just identify yourself to the police, so we*
> *know you are ok, so we can sight you, check on*
> *you, and simply close the book on this altogether.*

I tend to believe a lot of things that I'm told. My eldest son Joel says, 'I've got a problem with being gullible like that'. I believe in people too much. I believed this officer, so I agreed to meet a Nelson patrol car at the end of the street by a Petrol Station, you know, for them to sight me. Again, my drinking was in a survival mode of control so, as it was still early in the morning, I was smart enough to be sober. True, they met me, they sighted me, and then they placed me in the back of the car and took me to Nelson Police Station.

I sat in a holding area while they tried to make heads and tails of what they were meant to do with me. For the first time and many times after that, I learned that the police didn't really have a clue what the AOD Act of 1966 was. The way they kept talking about the Mental Health Act was really beginning to make me break into a sweat. I was picturing myself being taken off to a Psych ward somewhere and locked up until this could be figured out. Out of sheer panic, I gave them Joy's number after calls to the Police in Christchurch weren't shedding any further light on what the hell they were meant to do with me.

Joy must have been thrilled that they had me, so much so she told them to take me to Nelson A&E while she worked out how to get me back to Christchurch. They clearly couldn't hold me in the cells for an old speeding ticket and the drunk driving charge that showed on my record, so off to the hospital we went. It would have been comical if it wasn't my freedom at stake. Two policemen tried to make the hospital staff admit me with no presentation of a medical condition.

What they did, in the end, was to allow the police enter the locked door section of the emergency department where we all sat and looked at each other for the following few hours. Eventually, the policemen just got up and left me there. Later, the shifts changed, and the new staff inquired why I was sitting there. They decided to let me go, and I was allowed out of the locked doors to my freedom again.

I nearly ended up back in ER about 20 minutes later. I walked outside and down around to a hospital park area to have a cigarette and try and calm my panicking heart. The close call and the total loss of control of my choices coupled with being locked up for so long without any easy path of escape really set off an uncontrollable panic attack, and I passed out hitting my head on the way down. Someone must have seen the show and called the hospital staff. It was the first time, but not the last, that this would happen to me. While they were trying to get me in a wheelchair, I was madly talking as I crafted a lie about why I passed out. I used my heart condition as an excuse; I knew enough fancy cardiology words to make them believe I knew what I was talking about. I assured them that I knew why I'd fainted and that I'd be ok. And then I ran away from there.

I now understood that Joy meant business and that to keep my freedom, I needed to go a little further afield until someone got sick of chasing me. Either Joy or the police—one of them had to give up on me.

I didn't return to my friend's house, as Joy had put two and two together and worked out that I was staying at his home. As he was still under the two-year statutory hold under the act, he was threatened with having his butt hauled back with mine if he sheltered me. So, I left my clothes at his house, found a place to stay for that night, and made my way back to Wellington quietly and quickly as I could the next day.

I moved around a bit after that taking in some sights of the Lower North Island. I was worried that the police could trace me to my rental house. I really didn't want to lose that home and the security I had made for myself.

The police didn't give up the search. They started to really harass Barb; they started to bother her by regularly knocking on her door at 3 and 4 am demanding to know where I was. It was upsetting her and her children including the one I was later to become Godmother too. I knew the game was almost up. I couldn't continue to have her protect me at the detriment of her wellness and the wellness of her children. I promised her I'd turn myself in at the Lower Hutt Police Station as soon as I could get some important matters in order. Even as I write these words, I have to smile, turning myself in to the police, are not words or actions I could ever have foreseen happening in my old life.

I contacted the police in Christchurch again, asked for the policeman by name, and told him that I would present myself at Lower Hutt Station if he could assure me that I'd be sighted and allowed to go home. Just as he promised me last time, he promised me this time, and again I believed him. He told me there really wasn't anything they could do with me and that the Act was rarely enforced unless I'd been at risk of harm to myself or I'd harmed others. There were no others; I hadn't spoken to anyone other than my worried parents to assure them I was ok. How they knew I'd run in the first place didn't sink until much later.

The morning I went to the Lower Hutt station, I made appointments to visit a community law firm first and an AOD advocate second. I told my story to them both. I explained that I never harmed myself or others while under the influence of alcohol. I could have mentioned the only harm I caused people was telling them I loved them till their ears fell off as that was pretty much the way I behaved when I was drinking. I was a happy 'love drunk' rather than a 'hate the world' model.

They didn't really believe me when I spoke to them about the lack of care that Nova offered; about how I was just locked in there with no clear date of when I could leave; how I felt myself really slipping into a horrible feeling of entrapment and suppression. Nobody ever believed any of us 'inmates' when we talked about what Nova was like to our family or our friends. It was long before this day where I learned that people with addictions don't have a voice.

I agreed to present myself at the station, do as requested of me for a wellness check, and all should be ok.

It wasn't.

It was clear that things were not going to come up rosy after about the first 15 minutes. For some reason, I hadn't learned my lesson since the last time I trusted the police. True, I was an alcoholic, but that wasn't illegal. I had two drunk driving charges that I was deeply ashamed of, to the extent that I didn't drive a car again for years after I was able to get my license back. I was a good person, and I believed in doing right by others. I lived by a 'pay it forward' principle. I thought that all of these things I calculated about myself was evidence I'd be going home soon with my unopened favorite wine I had stashed in my backpack, along with a great selection of cheeses to celebrate finally having the cops and Joy off my back. I thought I would finally be free.

Quite the opposite happened.

The first words the sergeant at the station said to me were, "I don't know what you are talking about. I don't know anything about the AOD Act." It was like I was almost an annoyance to him. He wanted to know what illegal act I had committed to be under this AOD Act. Well… try and tell a cop you've done nothing wrong except drink too much of your fair share of fine wines which landed you under a government Act and see how that goes down. He didn't believe me. I told him about Christchurch Comms, about the phone calls that should have been made, that I was standing in front of him, (well-dressed, physically well presented, and well-spoken) to be given a wellness check and be allowed to go home. That just started to wind him even more, as now I was telling him how to do his job.

He told me to wait while he made some calls. He even allowed me to wait outside when I asked so I could have an incredibly nervous ciggie. Joel's assessment of me was proving to be right again. Why do I always believe in the good in people and trust what they say?

I stood outside the station about to walk back in when two decent sized policemen walked towards me and asked me to come with them.

I knew I was in it, not thinking for one minute what was about to happen could possibly ever happen in New Zealand—but it did.

I was escorted for the second time in around six weeks into a holding area. The panic was starting to rise as I was once again trapped. The same policeman from the front desk came out to tell me I would be held in their custody due to breaching the AOD Act. My shoes were taken from me, my bags were searched as was my body. The bottle of my favorite wine was discovered to which he replied coldly, "So, you're clearly an alcoholic, carrying around a bottle of wine in your bag." It was really a pitiful moment. Under the Act of 1966, I wasn't allowed to be in the possession of alcohol, not that I imagined he had sat down and read the Act written nearly 50 years ago. But Joy knew it and she had likely brought him up to speed so that she could legally use it against me to get me back in her prison.

I was taken to a cell, one with a glass partition which I found out later was like that so they were able to watch me if I were to harm myself. I've done many things, but I've never wanted to harm myself nor anyone around me. It was here that the next huge wave of panic set in. It started with my heart speeding up—the first signs that anxiety was striking. But this time was especially bad. It was doing a really awful dance rhythm this time, stopping long enough as the blood collected behind the prolapsed valve to give me a really decent head rush, then going a hundred miles an hour to catch up with the blood flow and rhythm again. This, in turn, set off another beauty of a panic attack.

It was something I was so used to and had always been able to successfully manage as long as I got something cold on my body. The only cold thing there was the concrete floor, so I literally stripped off my top down to my singlet top and lay on the floor, pressing my wrists and temples to the cold service. Again, the policeman that I first spoke to, must have walked past me or seen it on the cameras, or whatever happens inside police cells, and entered the cell. I'll never forget his words:

> *I've got a family member who's an alcoholic*
> *just like you, I know all the tricks, you're faking*
> *something to get yourself to a hospital so you can*
> *run, and that's not happening, so live with it.*

I really didn't give a fuck what he thought or said right there and then. I was too busy thinking about how I could slow down what was going on with me. It was later that it really sunk in; an addict is nothing when they carry that label. I didn't have any rights. Medically, I was treated like a leper. Morally, I was a reject. And verbally, I was screaming so loudly in silence that it was becoming almost impossible to live inside my head.

As it happened, around the same time, an ambulance medic walked into the cell. I don't know why, he may have been there treating someone else, but when he bent down and asked me what was wrong, I burst into tears. Again, for me to show that kind of emotion was rare, but he didn't know that. It was simply that someone was being kind to me, and it opened a trapped Niagara Falls that had been shut off inside my head.

I explained the heart condition I had, still doing my normal and trying to play it down. It was something I can usually handle. To this day, it is just something I live with. I explained that anxiety and the panic of being trapped brought it on, making it worse than normal sometimes. He quickly went out and returned with a portable ECG and was able to get a clear picture of what my heart was doing.

That kind man sat with me in that cell, talking to me like I was a human and not just an alcoholic. He got me some ice to help slow everything down, and some cold water to drink. Eventually, everything returned to normal. I've never had another attack like that one since, nor do I ever want to be placed in a cell where the possibility of it happening again would be high.

It was the first time that I had been locked up like that, but if being held in that glass cell wasn't bad enough, I was about to experience way worse.

A few hours after everything had slowed and calmed down, another kind human in uniform came and asked me if I'd like to go outside with him to have a cigarette. They had my bag, so they knew I smoked; they had my police record, so they knew I wasn't a risk. He took me outside for some fresh air and a ciggie. I know when I write that I have a funny heart that it sounds wrong that I smoke. But believe me, cigarettes at this stage in my life were the very least of my problems.

He gave me the news while I was standing outside with him, that I was to be police-escorted on a flight to Christchurch that night with a policeman that travelled criminals as part of his job. I would be handed over in Christchurch to the police there where I'd spend the night in the police cells in the center of the city. I asked him a question weirdly why I was processing all this fucking information, "Like really? Is the central police station still standing?" Once I got there, I realized why. They were dungeons like something out of some old medieval horror movies.

He was upfront and spot on with the information he gave me. He left out that I would be handcuffed in the police car on the ride to the airport, lead thru the airport handcuffed, escorted on the plane handcuffed, and that the Christchurch police would drive the police car onto the tarmac to the steps of the plane to take care of the handover. I swear the other passengers must have dined for weeks on the speculation of this serious criminal that was transported with them that night.

I felt that the pilot should have made an announcement to put everyone at ease, "Be calm and carry on, we've just got a woman here who's medicating her sorry life away by drinking far too much fine wine."

The policeman who escorted me was kind enough to take the cuffs off me when we were making the short trip. He too commented, "I really don't get it, is there something that's missing from your file? I've had a look at that AOD act which seems extremely outdated, but still, I can't really understand what you and I are doing here."

Even today, although it's exceedingly rare for me to rehash the baggage of my past when I tell someone this story, they will always ask the same thing, 'Come on, what else did you do to get treated like that?' My answer is always the same, I had an unhealthy love for fine wine. That was the story then. That's only part of the story now.

The next handover team also took pity on me. Halfway to the Christchurch Central Police Station, they stopped so I could have a ciggie. They too asked what I had really done, that there must be more to this. It seemed precious few people knew what the AOD Act of 1966 was, but they had heard of Nova.

I was bloody exhausted by this stage. It was late at night, I was really cold, and I hadn't been allowed to return to my house to collect any of my things. I suspect that even being escorted by the police, I would have turned it down anyway. I was pretty certain that I was about to lose another collection of belongings along with that rented room in that nice house in the Wellington Burbs.

I was expecting the same version of a cell that I'd just come from. I could feel the silent scream of "Nooooo!" welling up inside me at the knowledge that even police cells have basements.

I remember it was a Thursday night, and, although I was a first timer at all of this, I figured out pretty quickly that it was a busy night at that old station. It was a solid old building that had withstood the test of the quakes. Awake all night, I became more and more traumatized by the vicious fighting that was going on between the people in the cells around me, and I spent the entire night mentally trying to escape this sublevel of hell.

I was living my worst nightmare on repeat for a good part of ten hours listening to people talk about what they would do to each other when they got out, including partners and kids. Then the head-bashing started - one guy, bashing his head constantly against the door.

I was dressed for the lawyers and the advocate who were soundly tucked in their warm beds in Wellington. I wore clothes that suited the city vibe, not the freezing bloody cells in the depths of the Christchurch Central Police station.

Around 8 am, a policewoman came down and asked if I'd like to take part in an AOD survey that was funded by the government and actioned by a university (I think). I didn't have to participate, but if I did, I got juice and chocolate. I would have preferred her to say this had all been a big mistake and I could leave. But that wasn't on the cards.

This is how I found out that the government does a study every three to four years to gather statistics on where New Zealand is standing when it comes to our issue with addiction. Police cells and prisons are where they begin their examination; as if anyone is going to tell the truth about their addictions in either one of these places. So, I participated, I lied, and I got chocolate. Whoop Dee bloody do.

Joy turned up with another office staff member at about 10 am. There was clearly no rush to get me out of police cells because I must have deserved every second of the treatment I was receiving. The figure to get me back to Nova must have been huge. I think the police escort cost alone was around $3000 but I can't be sure.

Joy rocked up there and asked if I'd like to go for a coffee. I wanted to say so many things to her, but all that came out of my mouth was, "WHY?" I really can't remember her answer, because whatever came out of her mouth was just stupid fucking noise to me now.

After that, I just stayed silent. I expected to be going directly back to stealer of souls—Nova—but instead, they took me directly to visit the staff at Kennedy for the third time. I tried to tell everyone that would listen that I did not need a detox. My alcohol breath test at the Hutt Police Station had been negative nearly 24 hours ago, and I hadn't been drinking enough for a medically monitored withdrawal detox. No one listened and I spent another 14 days in the care of the kind and now very well-acquainted staff at Kennedy. I don't agree with myself taking or giving someone benzodiazepine if they don't require it, so I sat there and I sat there, and I thought to myself:

*What the hell next Denise. I think this*
*time, you are really, really DONE.*

CHAPTER 17

# *Bella Domani*

As I reach back in time, I know that there has always been a deep core of belief and faith in my heart and soul. Evidence of this happened as a result of an opportunity that was presented to my son.

Joel, my eldest son, came running in the door from school beside himself with excitement. He had received a phone call while at school telling him he had been selected for the New Zealand Junior Snowboard Team.

He had been competing and winning in his snowboard disciplines, boardercross being the strongest. (It's like motocross on snow.) Competitors have to have guts to be part of boardercross as it meant they would race around burns and jumps alongside three other males. I'd go and watch these events but spent much of the time with my eyes closed praying he wouldn't be hurt.

We had no idea that he was being considered for the team let alone the World Cup in France. But he was selected along with one other Queenstown girl, and he desperately wanted to go. Once the excitement wore off and I spoke with the head of the NZ Snowboard Association, the reality of the cost set in—around $15,000. It was a lot of money then. It still is now. We had a new business, we had mortgages, and I had a lot of other kids to consider. What was worse was that we had only three weeks to come up with it.

As all parents will understand, when it comes to your children, you'll walk over burning coals to make important things happen for them. I sat and thought about it for a day. Then while I was doing laundry, I came up with an idea. I believed I could make it happen, so I did make it happen.

I arranged a fundraiser at the local and popular Lone Star Restaurant. I set about spending long hours of the day calling in all favors by ringing every person I knew in Queenstown to donate a product or event for an auction. Joel was a popular kid, easy to like, and with a beautiful nature, which he carried with him through to adulthood and beyond. The people of the Southern lakes, my family, and my friends responded so generously that the night was a huge success raising well over our estimated target of $30,000. Joel went to France and competed in what was to be the first of many years of World Cups. He ranked well on the snowboard world rankings the first year and continued to his last World Cup that was held on home soil in the mountains of our home region where it all started. That last Snowboard World Cup Joel competed in, he was placed first in boardercross and second in the world overall.

I continued with this fundraising event every year, with more families coming on board to help with fundraising as more teenagers around the Southern lake's region were selected. Every year we would raise more and more funds to support our kids in their love for the sport of snowboarding.

Joel soon started picking up fantastic sponsors that supplied all his gear for years. The other children loved that (as did we as parents). We never needed to buy any boards, or snow clothes again. Every season, the latest and greatest gear arrived, so the children automatically have last year's items at their disposal to choose from. PlayStation came on board as a monetary sponsor, so the funds raised from those yearly auctions at the Lonestar Restaurant were able to be spread around families just like ours, with teenagers who were just starting out.

The next year I, along with the mother of another of Joel's teammates, Pania, travelled to the northern tip of Italy to a town called Sappada in the province of Udine with the 15 members of the

NZ Junior Snowboard Team. Pania and I had become firm friends over time with our boys' common interest in boarding making them good mates. I'll never forget waking up after almost 36 hours of travel at the NZ Teams  hotel. I pulled back the shutters to see the massive, magnificent presence of the Dolomites towering over me. That picture of those mighty mountains was a place I went back to in my head so many times when I needed to find a happy place in my Nova days.

The hotel was owned and run by an entire family, with Mama clearly the one in charge. She was a tiny little lady who carried an air of you-don't-want-to-mess-with-me. Pania and I decided that we would make amazing lunches for our team every day by slaving in the kitchen the night before. We turned out Kiwi Kai that was the envy of all the other world teams in the mountain huts at lunchtime. If I thought I knew how to cook for a horde, I had nothing on Pania.

Firstly, this meant getting past Mama to get into her kitchen. The language was a barrier; I had basic Italian, and Pania had none. The conversation was conveyed by actions, warm smiling eyes, hand gestures, and as the Italians do, a lot of touching and show of affection. We got into her kitchen by conversing with that kind of universal body language.

The first time, she walked up to me, stood on her tippy toes, grabbed my face in both her hands, looked me in the eye, and said, "Bella Domani," I thought our nights in her kitchen were over. She did it with such intensity, I didn't know if I'd upset her, made her happy, or what. I knew Bella was beautiful, but Domani wasn't on top of my common Italian words to use list.

She did this to me the next evening and the next, always grabbing my face in her hands and sending an intense message with her eyes. I eventually got to know her son and asked him to interpret it for me. He told me she was telling me in a very affectionate and meaningful way to have beautiful tomorrows. He said it wasn't like her to single a foreigner out like that, but that she must have seen something in me that needed to be affirmed.

If you believe you can truly make something happen that is important to you and to those you love, you will. You don't give up, you look in the corners, you check the shadows, and you explore all those hidden areas that are not in front of you. In short, you find a way. I made Joel's teenage years and his love for snowboarding possible after that one evening down in the laundry stressing over how I could get him to France. With a lightbulb moment and the idea of making this a community thing, I believed I could connect everyone together to make this a reality. I met with resistance, others thought I couldn't get enough funds together in time, and some thought that the community wouldn't give that easily. But I'm not that good at sitting down when I feel something so passionately. I knew this could really fly. If you want something bad enough, just believe you can make it happen, then get to work to make sure it does.

Mama's message while her seasoned hands were cupping my face never left me either. I had a lifetime of beautiful tomorrows in front of me back when I had a life—back when the old me used to dream and used to matter.

Fifteen years after I was first given Mama's message, and on the day of the anniversary of my one year of choosing life over the bottle, I went and had that little old Italian Mama's words tattooed on the inside of my drinking arm. What it stood for then at one year sober and what it stands for today, years later, carries the same message to me. If I just don't lift that arm to my mouth with a glass of alcohol attached to it, I will always have Bella Domani—a Beautiful Tomorrow.

C HAPTER 18

# *First, I fight for freedom*

Maybe it had been my six weeks of semi-freedom, of living in control of my choices, good and bad, but my choices nonetheless, or maybe it was that while I was out, I'd held back on donating all my money to Stoneleigh winery's coffers, but I had some fight in me. I didn't know where this fight had come from or how I would use it. But there was no doubt that it was there.

I heard stories from the girls at Nova that my parents had been contacted. Fair enough. I heard from the staff themselves, one more than others who was smirking that she knew all about me, that my now, very ex-husband had been working with Joy to find me. That was how she was getting the intel she needed to track me down. I also learned from Nelly and Karen, who weren't in the shadows, that they had been contacted by the mental health worker who suggested this hell hole, to begin with, and that's how they knew what I'd done and how I was back.

For the first time in my life, but definitely, not for the last, I slowed everything down, and I waited. My old personality was to react there and then, to get angry, or get sad, not to think things through, and not to wait 24 hours or longer to let the initial emotion pass and let the real ones settle in. This time, I elected to be calm so I could have some clarity.

I waited until Joy felt comfortable that I wasn't planning to run. I did lots of research around the privacy act, and I made phone calls to advocates to learn my privacy rights. I went to the Nova front office many weeks later, and I asked the sweet girl there if I could have copies of all my paperwork that I signed when I arrived back this last time and from all the times of admissions past. It raised suspicion, but I wasn't surprised. She had to check with Joy first. But I did know my rights that I was entitled to a copy. I made up some bullshit story about how I was closing my casting company down and needed to show that I was in a government establishment, blah blah. In the end, I got what I needed. It should have been an instant hand over, but it took a few more weeks before they complied and released the paperwork.

And did my heart sing when I got those papers in my hands? What I was after were the confidentiality parts. Who were they allowed to talk to regarding my welfare, and who couldn't they disclose my information to? I had left it totally blank with a big fat line drawn through where any names should be placed. I'd also written, every time, "No one." I remember also verbally saying each time to Joy that I did not want my now-ex to be told anything about me. We had long ago stopped having anything to do with each other. Other than communication via email regarding our youngest, we never spoke. It suited both of us by then.

The reason for a confidentiality agreement is that a person who is under the care of a treatment facility is entitled to have nonentity status. They can stipulate who can or cannot know if a person is even checked into a facility. You can imagine the effect that it would have on a person who had gone to a real Rehab if the world was able to call up and find out they were there. Even worse, they should never be given private information about that person, their actions, and the rehab's opinion of their current presentation.

Joy had too much confidence (or arrogance) in her role and her job. What she thought and said went. No questions. There were, however, rules that couldn't be broken and, if taken to the right organisation, couldn't be overlooked.

She repeatedly told people that I just couldn't help myself, that I had come back drunk, and, because I didn't want to conform to the rules, that I had thrown my toys out of the cot. This is what alcoholics do—they throw their toys out of their cot. She liked that saying much to her detriment because I'd heard it often, and I was hearing it from all those that she had contacted, the ex-husband included. Joy had stayed in touch with him throughout that time of my so-called run for freedom. This much I knew was true. I just had to prove it.

So, I waited, and when I thought that the mask of resignation I wore had become clear to everyone, I made an appointment, and I went to see her. I credit my stellar performance to my years behind the camera, guiding people to act out a character that they were not natural with, along with the old placid me thrown in there to play out the part of a grateful, apologetic, resigned woman, who just wanted to make amends with her for the trouble I had caused.

I now know this is called "motivational interviewing." I avoided any argument and direct resistance or confrontation, and I expressed empathy through really reflective listening. I listened and nodded while she proceeded to tell me that she had long conversations with my ex-husband about me, how she'd told him I had just thrown my toys out of the cot, how she'd spoken to all these others (friends, family) to find me and make sure I was safe. I again apologised for the trouble I caused her, thanked her for having the energy to keep looking for me, and for bringing me back.

Then I got up and I walked out of that office, and I turned off the mini recording device I'd been holding in my hand.

# CHAPTER 19

# *The Final Days*

I t didn't take long till my freedom was finally officially secured. I went through the right channels. I waited. Then I sent the transcript of the recording to the right place, and I waited. The few close girls who had remained trapped with me through all those long Nova days and nights also waited. We kept silent and we waited. I couldn't tell you what date it was, but spring was in the air. I received the letter from the right government department on the same day that Joy did. I was already packed when she came down to my room. I can barely remember the words she used, but I'll never forget the look on her face. I had a choice of either going ahead with legal charges, or I was to be immediately discharged from under the AOD Act of 19 bloody 66.

*It was truly over Nova. You may have had
a chance in changing people's lives. If you
put more research and resources into actually
helping people with the illness of the disease
of addiction, rather than trapping people. At
the very least to give them respect rather than
punish people suffering such unwellness.
There was no hope inside your walls that any
one person could overcome substance abuse,
let alone leave with some form of education*

*around addiction. No hope and no promise*
*of a different future. These words are not*
*part of your vocabulary. Rather, you gloated*
*about how many people your fucked-up*
*establishment would see come back again*
*through your bloody revolving doors.*

I lost touch with most of the people I'd spent a good part of over a year within that hellhole. Some became Facebook friends and we communicated when their names would pop up on my feed or when family and friends posted their memories of them and details of their funerals.

That revolving door hellhole place called Nova stole a part of my life that took a long time and really good professional help to remove from my memory bank and release. Most people just didn't believe me that the place could be this bad–that a place like this could exist in New Zealand today. Well, it did and still does, although I don't know who is in charge or how it runs today. Their website seems to give the same glowing ideation of a lovely farm with lots of resources, which in 2011/12 was most certainly not what was offered.

Nova caused me great harm. It dismissed and diminished me as a person. I was treated as a criminal, not an unwell person with an illness. It kept me running from rehabs or any decent help for a further two years, fearing every place that family and friends found for me would just be a repeat of Nova. I always said that I was going to expose that place one day, somehow, someway. So, I waited and here it is.

*Now I'm truly finally done with*
*you, it's over, Nova.*

People who consider giving up on whatever substance they are addicted to enter into a really horrible stage of letting go of what has made them feel good. They cling to an establishment or support people that will offer good professional help. It's a link that takes them from letting go to grabbing on. People who take a chance on this, but end up in a badly run, unprofessional facility, will undoubtedly return to the substance that made them feel better. They will fall harder and heavier than before. Therefore, coming so close to letting go and not receiving the correct care will drive almost everyone to distance themselves from any other establishment for a long time afterward. In some cases, the length of time and the distance between good care can be and often is fatal as it was for many that passed through the gates of hell that were Nova's revolving doors.

# CHAPTER 20

# *Purgatory*

For the next two years of my life, I tried to function as normal as normal should be. I moved back to Wellington and soon after I moved out of that rental in the burbs. I hammered the bottle, to begin with, but started to realize I wasn't in a race to get numb anymore. So, I pulled the handbrake up a notch, just ever so slightly.

I think it was becoming clear to the fireman that not all was what it seemed with me, and so I had to do what I'd become accustomed to doing and move on—on to new people and places where no one knew me and where there was no knowledge that I loved a wine at night, and where no one was aware that it controlled my every waking move and thought.

I found a nice house with a nice man in another suburb, closer to Jack's school, with his son in the same school just a year ahead. I'd chosen to really moderate my intake of alcohol by only drinking enough in the mornings to stop the shakes, a little at lunchtime to comfortably forget what I'd become, and a decent amount at night to knock myself out.

The nice man had a good job, a nice house, and a similar addiction to mine, so we suited and liked each other eventually falling into a convenient relationship. Did I use him? Yes! I didn't mean to, but looking back, I did. He wanted more from me, but I didn't know who the "me" was, so I was completely incapable of giving him something that didn't really exist other than how to get to the supermarket to get wine and how to get back.

I'd go in the morning, walking in the early days until I couldn't make it there that way anymore with my shopping bag over my arm. I'd go to different supermarkets, and I would buy the daily newspaper and bacon. I'd also buy a roast or a corned beef that I'd tell the checkout chick I was going to be slowly cooking for guests that night. And I'd buy a minimum of 5 bottles of fine wine because I was having a dinner party. I kept up the ruse so they would not know there was one person at my dinner party: me. Many weeks passed with this charade. The bacon and roast wouldn't make it home; the freezer was full of my cover-ups. I'd walk out of the supermarket and throw the whole lot in the bin. The paper would stay because it stopped the bottles banging together and, heaven forbid, breaking. I had a problem with getting rid of all the bottles due to our recycling bin only holding so much glass. So, the night before collection, I would wander down the street, generously donating a few empties here and a few empties there to our neighbors' recycling bins. As I did, I would occasionally be thinking of a neighbor, "Aww, Number 135, you've got a similar problem to mine."

I lived for the weekends and holidays when I'd spend time with my son. The times that I had Jack, which was most weekends, were cherished, so I remained sober. My sober was different from other people's sober. As time marched on and my liver was searching for another guardian angel to help it out, my need for alcohol wasn't to get happy, or numb—it was simply a means to get normal.

If I had two glasses in the morning, all I felt was normal again, normal enough to function. I was chemically dependent on the best friend I'd ever known. It may have owned me, but I thought I could control it. Till I couldn't anymore.

Weirdly, I have some good memories of the first twelve months I lived in that nice house with that nice man. Jack will say now, as an adult, he doesn't really ever remember seeing me drunk, he was just always told that I was one. He did slice open an emotional wound that needed to be addressed much later when I was finally sober when he told me that the first time he learned not to trust me was when I told him I didn't drink anymore, but he caught me dragging a bottle of wine out of the laundry cupboard.

In August 2013, I was watching ads on TV for island getaways to Rarotonga. So, I did some fast research, rang my eldest son Joel in Australia, and arranged for us to meet at Auckland airport where we would both fly off together to the sun for a week. Both his father, Greg, Joel, and I are genetically connected when it comes to choosing to do something fun. We are fully spontaneous. Why wait? Let's pack the car and do it now.

I was excited about the trip. I hadn't seen Joel in a long time—maybe about a year. He lived in Aussie making a good life for himself. We were so close, he and I. Our age difference of 20 years meant that, in a way, we had grown up together, especially in the early days of what we called Park St. life. We lived there for ten years with lovely flat mates now and again, and one serious boyfriend, the only other true love in my life, Greg Young, who was with us off and on for five years, before life happened and he sadly moved on. At Park St, Joel was an only child, happily growing as a young boy, just him and his Mum. We stayed that way until our new family came along.

He choked up when he first saw me, and I know when he says, "Oh, Mum," something has got to be wrong. It was the shape of me that startled him. I'd lost huge amounts of weight in the previous year. My joy of seeing him immediately crashed into sadness. The look in his eyes while he tried not to tear up and the sound of his voice breaking while trying so hard to be strong, was more than I could bear.

Of course, Joel had been told that I had it all under control these days. None of us knew enough about alcoholism to realize that the concept of 'under control' is a myth and a lie. I'd recently started having bad lower and side back pain, which later on I was to discover was my liver and kidneys telling me they were getting their bags packed and preparing to turn the lights out.

I stood in Departures beside Joel, and then suddenly I wasn't. I woke up on the ground looking at him and looking at security. To this day, that look on Joel's face haunts me, and I never want to see it again. Nor have I ever forgotten his words, "Oh Mum, we're not going anywhere."

Even writing this while taking myself back to that day really upsets me. But it was and still is a visual and verbal memory scar that has stopped me many a time when the thought of going back to where I've come from raised its ugly head in the early days of struggling to make it over to the other side.

I don't know how I did it, but as I did the day in the hospital park in Nelson, I was able to bounce up and quickly use some elaborate obviously believable story that allowed us to carry on and board our flight to the Pacific Islands.

It was there that I started to hear little pieces of what I'd been doing and saying to Joel over the last year or so when I made drunk phone calls to him. He shared how much my alcoholic actions were really taking a toll on his mental health. He told me his anxiety levels went up fast when he saw I was calling and that he was struggling to cope with worrying about me all the time. He made it clear that I wasn't fooling him ever with my lies around alcohol that he could tell as soon as I spoke when I'd been drinking and drinking too much. He asked me to try and contain it while we were on the island, try and learn to start controlling it, and to have a good time, but to pace myself. Little did we know it was all a little late for that.

I did control it to a point of doable while we spent a week, then extended it to two weeks, and then three lovely weeks on that island. If my eyes leak with memories of damage that I've done, they also leak of memories of a time that we would probably never have again. It was three beautiful weeks of sun, combined with our love for snorkeling. We laughed, we were close, and I was a mother until I was not.

The first time I felt that I may be in trouble health-wise was when I was on that pacific island with Joel. My passing out had scared me much more than I'd let on to Joel at the time. I'd used the excuse of being tired and my disco beating banging heart plus other bullshit to cover it up and make him less concerned about me.

Some nights, even with the sedative from alcohol flowing through my veins, I'd have a lot of pain in my back. But the mornings were when the pain was almost unbearable until I drank, coupled with constant pins and needles and muscle pain that I would later learn was Alcohol Neuropathy. My muscles ached from dehydration and electrolyte imbalance, although I learned somewhere to try and hydrate my body with extra electrolytes. I was always tired, but pretending I wasn't, I couldn't stomach any food, which Joel noticed and constantly tried to make me eat.

For the first time, in the early dark witching hours on that Island where good memories were being made with my eldest son and me, I was coming to the realization that while I was mentally capable of keeping this thirst for alcoholic numbness up, my organs were very strongly suggesting that they'd had enough. I was physically feeling darkness I had no desire to greet. But it was creeping nearer.

I returned home to New Zealand and carried on just like before. The feeling that I'd lost a battle I only half fought against the bottle was clear and present with me every day. It still didn't stop me. I used alcohol more and more in the morning, lying to myself that my organs just need their happy juice, and, momentarily, they would be ok. The pain would go, and I'd carry on my day as per normal, on repeat. I could no longer walk to the supermarket, so instead, I called a taxi. I used to dread it when a minivan cab would turn up, because launching myself into the front passenger seat was too hard or trying to open the back door required too much strength.

I had another bright idea that maybe going to stay with Joel in Australia would help curb my need for four bottles a day, and possibly by being around him, I could drop to three, or even only the two that I needed to function on to be normal.

It didn't work, I just bled my alcoholism all over Joel even more. I embarrassed him by embracing his friends while drunk, so Joel stopped them coming. By the time his godmother Susan showed up for a holiday and a sneak look of what returning to Aussie might look like for her, I'd moved out from Joel's apartment into a hotel apartment down the road.

Susan was another who got a shock when she saw me, but, seriously and sadly, my presentation was overshadowed by her sore leg and feeling of tiredness the entire time. We still had a really nice time together; my best friend and I did what we could under both our health-related circumstances and did what we could just like all the other holidays that we had been taking together for years.

She and I were to leave Queensland on the same flight home in late November 2013. I did my normal, and for the third time, I dropped and woke up on the airport floor. This time was different, and it really annoyed me. I hadn't been drinking a lot that day, nor the night before, and definitely not my normal levels of organ juice anyway. I sat inside the airport for a good part of an hour before we cleared customs as it was hot, and I needed to be cold. My body was sending me signals that I felt loud and clear, but my brain just wasn't computing. I had to stay and get cleared to fly by a doctor the next day, and Susan went on that flight home to eventually receive the cancer diagnosis a month later.

One last significant event happened in February 2014. I flew to Queenstown to attend the wedding of Andi's son Adam to his long-time love, Michael. I'd watched Adam grow from two years old, so his wedding was a huge event that I'd been looking forward too. I also remember thinking that this may be a chance for Andi, Tanya, and I to finally catch up and for me to try and offer some kind of apology to repair all of the damage I had done to our friendship. We had never really talked about it, so for me, this presented a golden opportunity.

I was severely unwell in my thoughts. By now, drinking six bottles of wine a day, my hair had all but fallen out, my teeth had started to crumble due to vomiting up everything that I put in. Food had long ago been crossed off the list of importance, so poached egg yolks constituted my entire diet. My excessively bloated face looked like a million bees had stung me and sat on top of an XXS small body. I was doubled over in pain almost 24/7 from excruciating pain in my stomach and back that had me sitting on the toilet with nothing coming out. Peeing stung me from urinary tract infections. My muscles ached and cramped. I oozed the smell of alcohol from my pores. I joked that I owned shares in a mints company as I sucked on tins of the things thinking this would cover the smell. Getting in the shower was a huge mission—it just took so much energy, it zapped me as the water stung my skin like a million needles being chucked at me.

I had this idea that, in this broken state, I could fly off to the wedding of a darling boy that I loved all his life and make up with his mother and my other best friend.

I just couldn't see it. I hadn't looked in the mirror for months, but still I just couldn't see what I'd become. I'd moved out of the nice man's house to a dark apartment on a monthly rental. So, I never saw the light of day unless it was to get to a shop that was all but next door to buy what I knew now to be my truly deadly enemy; Sav.

I went to Queenstown anyway, fell out of the plane again, and went home to Karen's where she promptly fed me enough of the poison to cleverly knock me out and went to the wedding without me. I woke up with my pretty size six dress beside me that I had to order online to get the smallest size. I jumped up, put it on, and went to Susan's looking for a party, which ended up being my sick sorry self, sitting there while Susan, who was dying, was crying and begging me to give the fucking alcohol up.

It didn't work. It registered in me then, through the eyes of those I love, that looked in horror at me that I was probably toast, So I promptly went back to Wellington and toasted to that. Not before the groom turned up, breaking down at the sight of me, and not without my beautiful friends begging me to let them try and get me into a rehab somewhere. I'm not sure if it was Nelly or Karen who asked me if I had my affairs in order. I was just sad, and tired—so bloody tired of being tired, and so over the struggle and fight of maintaining alcohol levels to cease the pain. I was so empty and broken, not knowing how the hell I arrived in this sublevel of hell. Not knowing anything anymore other than deep dark shame in every minute I was awake until blackout arrived, and the nightmares started.

I did what I always did—I booked an early flight and got out of Queenstown fast. It was a screaming match with Nelly and Karen, but my biggest fear was they would try and take my alcohol away. I clung to that like the death that we all knew was coming. We just didn't know when.

I went home to my dark dingy flat. Long gone was a nice home in the Wellington burbs. I climbed into bed and stayed there.

The girls had called the nice man, they didn't want me to die alone. So, he came and picked me up from the dark flat and took me back home with him. I didn't put up a fight, nor did he fight me drinking. He had decided enough was enough with alcohol himself a long while back and was doing well counting nearly six months sober.

I breathed, I swallowed, I slept, I repeated. I knew there was no going anywhere now, not physically, and not in my head. It was just silent screaming noise.

You may wonder why no one called an ambulance or called authorities. The simple fact is you can't. If I didn't want help, then they couldn't offer help. I was an alcoholic living corpse that no longer felt worthy of any help. It's amazing how our bodies are the first home that we know, but it's our psychological home that really determines how that home is respected. I could open my mouth and say I didn't want help because I truly believed that, after all these years, all the pain and suffering I had caused my children and parents, I deserved nothing more than what was coming to me.

I just wanted it to happen quickly and quietly, and without too much more pain.

I sat on the steps of his house a week or so after Queenstown, nursing my wine bottle. Long ago, I abandoned drinking from a glass because I would spill precious poison all over me. My shaking was permanent now. Alcohol did nothing but relieve the pain for a short while and put me to sleep. I neither got drunk from it nor was I ever sober. I was just breathing and existing.

While sitting there on those steps looking at nothing and thinking nothing, I got an unusual phone call from Joel. I thought that we had not spoken in a while. Unbeknownst to me, I called him regularly, normally around 3 am his time, but in my blackout that was my constant world, I had no memory of my calls to him.

He delivered these lifesaving words to me that day. I remember it like it was a minute ago. "I love you Mum, more than anything in this world, but I'm going to Thailand tomorrow, I'm changing my phone number, and I never want you to call me again".

And with that, I can honestly say, it was then in that moment that I felt what, 'truly, broken, nothingness, was.'

That phone call woke me up; it was like the last thread to my life was being cut.

*If I'd ever felt sick to my bones with events*
*and damage that I'd let my drinking lead to*
*before, this was mentally and physically the*
*ultimate mother lode shattering bomb*

So, there and then, I made a choice. I had to find a way to get cured of this for those that loved me, not for me. They were worthy of more than this, even if I felt I wasn't. Trouble was I was just a little too far gone towards the darkness to figure out how to claw my way back to the light.

# CHAPTER 21

# *The beginning of the end.*

I'd woken up one morning a few weeks back and had looked at a text on my phone from my dear friend, Saskia. She was Andi's sister and a wise old soul. She knew things in advance and felt things around her that couldn't be explained. The text read,

> *After what you said to me last night, I*
> *don't want to ever speak to you again.*

I tried to call her and ask who that text was meant for, but she wouldn't answer. Then I looked at my call log. It then registered that I may have said something horrible to her in a blackout. It had happened before with other friends who used to be there, and to this day I'll never know what I'd said to Saskia that night.

So, this morning a few weeks later when the phone rang and it was Saskia, I didn't expect what she was about to say. It was only a few days after Joel's final call to me, so in a way, I wasn't surprised that Sas showed up. It was in her nature to often just appear out of the abyss in times of troubled waters.

She said:

> *Denise, listen to me now, I know you think you*
> *are past anyone helping you now, and you think*
> *you're not worth it, but your children are. For*
> *the love of your children, you have got to at least*

> *try this one last time. I'm sending you a phone*
> *number of a place I've found for you. They are*
> *good people, they care. They know what you*
> *have is a disease, an illness, and they can help*
> *you. I promise you I've made sure of that. But*
> *you have to want it and you have to call them!*

So, I did.

I called this place. I didn't speak, I just listened. The nice voice on the phone said, "You just get yourself here, Denise. You're worthy of a chance. You may not feel it now, but I promise we will take care of you here until you do think you're worth better than this."

It was the sincerity of the words, "we will take care of you now" that registered more than anything.

I hung up and, for some reason, the three phone calls suddenly made me start to really sob for the first time in such a long, long time. I felt something stronger than self-hate; I felt Joel's pain, I felt Jack's pain. I felt scared for them. I felt what it must have been like for my parents and my friends watching and waiting as I just gave in.

In my unwell state of mind, I was damn sure I was no longer capable of help. I drank, and I became an alcoholic. I went to a rehab once that maybe could have helped but I didn't let it. I was locked up in another rehab that didn't count. Then I just caved into alcoholism. It was my reality, and it was my world that I had weakly folded myself into.

But my children, my family, were worth something better than this. They deserved better than this. They deserved better, even if I felt I didn't.

I closed my eyes, and I made a choice not to go towards the darkness of a long sleep, but to wake up and give myself another chance of beating this. So, for them I did.

It's like a tiny torch had been shone down a very deep dark hole in my mind, and a tiny step ladder had been offered to me. All I had to do was stand up, step up and head in the direction of that tiny light that offered some other way out of this other than death.

"They say a person needs just three things to be truly happy in this world: Someone to love, Something to do, and Something to hope for" – *Tom Bodett*

MY ELDEST SON "JOEL"

MY BABY BOY "JACKSON"

# MAKING HAPPY MEMORIES
# WITH MY BOYS

# "GREG, JOEL AND I"
# A FAMILY

# KIM AND MARK ON BOARD S/V ZIZI

# WITH NICK THE DAY HE FINALLY LEFT
# THAILAND, SEPT 2020

ANDI TANYA AND I
ANDIS WEDDING 1987

TANYA, ME, ANDI 30
YEARS LATER 2017

LIZZIE

SAM

## SUSAN AND I 2006

## ANDI AND I 2015

## JILLY

## SIMON

ME, KAREN AND NELLY 1 MONTH BEORE ENTERING REHAB
2014

ME, KAREN AND NELLY 3 MONTHS
SOBER JUNE 2014

## MY SOULS HOME, QUEENSTOWN, NEW ZEALAND

## KAT, GOOD TIMES. CHIANG MAI, THAILAND 2019

# CHAPTER 22

# *The day I met HOPE*

The nice man got me to the airport in Wellington about 12 hours after I phoned the nice voice on the phone back to say I was coming.

I really have no memory of it. It was the 6th of March 2014, my middle son from the heart's birthday. I landed in Auckland where a bright bubbly girl named Christine was waiting. I didn't know it then but she was a client not a staff member, part of the clever module that Capri Hospital had established; letting the clients introduce new people to the beginning of the end. She let me skull the last of my water bottle of wine, then held my hair while I threw it up in the rubbish bin.

I got in the car with her and a man who I thought must be the caretaker the way he talked about the place with such joy, while I sat there in silence not wanting to be noticed. I was starting to get scared of another detox that was just around the next bend, and rightfully so, as it was to be the mother of all detoxes. No matter how drugged up I was, it was a bitch! I just stayed there in that bed wanting to go to sleep and never wake up. I joke now with the sick sense of humor that comes from those of us that have been part of this club. I could survive another drink, but I'm bloody certain I couldn't survive another detox.

The nice voice on the phone, Michelle, met me when I arrived. She's one of life's angels on earth—so unbelievably kind, so compassionate, and at the same time so direct and honest that you trusted what she was saying immediately. No one crossed her when she meant business. Her business was all about waking up dead walking souls like me with straightforward honest statements and straight answers to what your chances of living are or not, if you don't make the right choice to chance help.

She didn't come from addiction, but she knew every inch of it. This place wasn't about addiction; it was all about how the hell you arrived at its deadly gates, to begin with. Michelle had a good background and firsthand professional knowledge of mental health, and in the four walls of this bubble that was a Rehab Hospital, that's what mattered more and that's what came first.

I stayed in my room for about two days before they made me get up and get on with the art of living. It took me a while to register that the staff in uniforms were nurses, real nurses and that they knew their craft. They were each so kind that every time one would lean in to hug me, I'd break. There was no judgment, just total honest understanding, care, and compassion.

There was a nurse on duty 24/7, always three during the day, and then one, sometimes two after 8 pm. Little Florence Nightingales everywhere. After 11 pm, they would creep into your room and check on you to make sure you were ok, on the hour every hour. I didn't know this until around day twenty when I awoke to see Ruth the nurse standing at the door. She explained they had been doing that every night just making sure I was sleeping gently.

They slowly started nursing me back to what resembled a human being. I had starved my body of nutrients and food for so long, I had to be fed liquids first, then slowly food was introduced. When someone hasn't eaten properly in a long time, there's a high risk of Re-Feeding syndrome occurring, so I had to be monitored with how and what I ate for the first two weeks.

My bright pink suitcase had been put on the plane in Wellington. The airport cameras had proven this because there was no way I could be sure, but my luggage didn't turn up in Auckland. I hadn't packed it or carried it, so I was pretty much in the dark of the mystery of the bag. Lovely, kind women who were out-patients at Capri Hospital would bring me in some of their old skinny clothes to wear. Sue, who was the owner of Capri, married to Guy who I thought was the caretaker in the pickup car, had gone out and purchased some warm clothes for me to wear until my pink suitcase turned up.

I mention this as it was the way I started to meet people at Capri, people who had been where I was and were now on their way forward to the life they had chosen for themselves. The outpatients had heard about the now-infamous lost pinky and knew what it must be like to turn up with nothing but your handbag. To be honest, a good part of the last 3 years had pretty much been just me and my handbag. Some brought in moisturizer or shampoo or lip balm, or a candle or card—little things they knew they would have wanted, little things that made me feel I mattered.

This enabled me to talk to people just like me, to hear them constantly reassure me I was in the right place, that they knew how I must be feeling, and to just hold on to any slither of courage I had, that it would get better.

Kindness, understanding, and connection helped give me hope. It took a while. Day 18 to be exact.

I signed the paperwork for Capri Hospital a few days later when I could read, the same way I had in Nova, but this time just a hell of a lot more professionally. I didn't want anyone to know where I was. Saskia had promised this. She kept her word, but the nice man had let others know I took a chance on life and had headed North.

On day 15, Pinky, my bag turned up via Australia. Everyone was so excited, they stood and cheered.

On day 16, a single sunflower arrived from my sister Robyn with a card saying,

*"We love you, Denise. Unconditional
love never dies."*

On day 17, the father of a past client who offered families of clients support at Capri and who I hadn't seen since around day 7, walked right past me. I was kind of hurt. But I said his name to call him back. Chris just turned and stared at me. My unwell mind was doing fast calculations to think when I'd upset him and how. Then I registered. I'd changed that dramatically from someone who looked like the walking dead, into someone who now glowed with life of the living; he simply had not recognized me. He was so excited to see me looking human again and told me so while hugging me.

I get to experience what Chris saw that day all the time now. How lucky am I? It is the thing I get most excited about when I'm returning to treatment clinics to see how my clients are doing. The glow of someone who is coming out of the darkness and finally being able to see the light shines externally so bright. It's the glow of health returning, but mostly it's a glow of hope. It's a turning point for me in this job and tells me I can breathe now—they are on their way.

On day 18, at Capri Hospital, I looked in the mirror for the first time in so, so long. I didn't recognize my face. I seriously didn't know who was staring back, but what I did see when I looked into my eyes was someone who wanted to live. Someone who wanted to have the chance to say, "I'm sorry." Someone who wanted to be a mother again, a daughter, a sister, and a friend. Someone who wanted a chance. Someone who had hope. This was the moment that time stood still. It was then that I decided, I'm done, I'm never ever going back to that enemy I called a friend for so long. Know what? I didn't. I just decided there and then, as I stared in that mirror at someone I didn't know.

*Denise, whoever you are, I believe I*
*want to fight this. So, I will.*

And that was the end of that part of my life. Now all I had to do was learn how to begin again.

CHAPTER. 23

# *Mental health matters*

Serious Addiction issues have statistically been evident in New Zealand for years and years. Studies done in 2015 showed that 10% of our population was affected by addictive substances. Mental health wasn't associated with addiction until only recently when the government decided to spend a year and a lot of money asking the people questions to work out that mental health had something to do with addiction.

It's a great thing that the government finally recognized that mental health had something to do with addiction. All of those working in this field had known this for years, and all those that suffer from Substance Use Disorder could have told them this in a heartbeat. However, they have only now started to understand and finally bloody acknowledge it.

Unwellness in mental health can lead to a person—any person, weak or strong, rich, or poor—to use and eventually rely on an addictive substance to self-medicate that person's mental health issues. It's been recognized by the mental and addiction community, as well as the health and medical professions worldwide for years. So why did it take our government FOREVER to put together a team of experts to travel the country for a year, to hear from the people to work it out? They only needed to collect 100 people who worked in AOD/MH together for a five-minute meeting, and they would have had enough facts to slap Mental Health onto the Addiction label years earlier.

Don't get me wrong, I'm mighty glad they have finally recognized it. But it begs the question; Now what are they going to do about it?

Anyone who has suffered from this knows one thing. You wouldn't wish addiction on your worst enemy. Yes, the question of choice is raised in an argument all the time. Until you have either lived it or lived with it, your opinion is simply not informed.

Not one human being decides that they are going to grow up, drink, and become an alcoholic or drug addict. In most cases, it evolves out of mental health issues that you either know you have or later when presented with professional psychological facts, learn to accept that you have. However, mental health is recognized as the leader in taking you towards the addiction pathway.

It evolves out of genetic disposition or it evolves out of social and economic and environmental circumstances. When it's done evolving, you find that you are chemically addicted and psychologically reliant on the substance and its effects to survive on a day to day basis. Sometimes just to feel.

It's one of the least understood diseases that exist. It's one that attacks all aspects of your life, causing you not only horrific physical and psychological damage, but spreads its ugly illness over the lives of everyone that encounters it, and tries to help you stop its path of destruction. It's a family, community, national, and international disease that oozes out of the person who suffers from it, capturing and hurting the people they love.

After the family has been affected, the community begins to feel the sting of it; employers that can no longer turn a blind eye, emergency services, hospitals, police, courts, prisons, and funeral homes get involved. Then the nation feels it with high costs for services. Lastly, the world feels it, because it's everywhere, hurting everyone. And it's only getting worse rather than better.

Addiction is seen as a weakness far more readily than understood, and is treated as a mental health/addiction, illness, and disease. It does have its own name and has for years in medical journals. It is listed in the Diagnostic and Statistical Manual of Mental Disorders

(DSM-5), a medical bible, addiction to a substance, alcohol, and drugs of any kind is called Substance Use Disorder. (SUD)

It's a monster. It's real. It can affect any one of us and, if left untreated, it most certainly kills. For example, the metaphor used in escaping from methamphetamine addiction is that people must choose institution, prison, or death. It goes for all substances and doesn't make any difference what brand we use to get there. We all meet at the same gates of addiction hell.

# CHAPTER 24

# *Shutting Down*

I never wanted to die, ever. I simply did not know how to live anymore. For a long time after, I'd look back on the last two years of my drinking and I wonder if I would have simply never awakened. Would I have made it? That's how weird the unwell mind works. I wouldn't have made it, but still, I often questioned it. That's how powerful the illness of addiction is. You keep thinking that this won't be the end, even when others like you are dying all around you. For a good part of 18 months, I'd think like that with nasty little thoughts sitting just outside my ear saying it wasn't all that bad. This hit me particularly hard in the face when, at one year sober, I had blood tests at the suggestion of my doctor just to see where my liver count stood.

When I arrived at Capri Hospital the year before in 2014, my clinician gave me some hard-hitting facts. My liver tests alone showed that it was weeks, if not days away from shutting down. In fact, it should have already happened. My liver count numbers were signalling the end. No second chance.

*Get it, Denise? Check! Got it!*

Your liver count should range between 0-50, in a healthy liver. Anything over 50, like 80, isn't good. So here a year later, my beautiful faithful liver had worked so hard to give me a second chance by showing my count had gone from 2018 to 17.  For a New York minute, I thought, "Brilliant, I can give it another shot now."

I don't blame you if you've read my story thus far and thought wow, you really are not that nice a person. I really, don't care. The chapters of my addiction years are before you for a reason. Not for you to like or dislike me, I just desperately want you to understand how it can all happen. How it could happen or has happened to you.  How it could happen to someone you love. My story, although unique to me, is just the same version of what is happening to millions upon millions of people around the world.

Look at a small country like New Zealand. We may be recognized as rugby world cup holders, a country that is doing great things trying to manage COVID, etc. but on the world scale, we are second in the modern world per head of population for the highest number of meth users. Although Meth is talked and read about more than alcohol due to its illegal status and criminal activity associated with the substance, alcohol is still the number one killer.

I'm not going to make excuses, I've made enough of them to last a lifetime, but what I am going to say, was that I spent a good part of those 28 days as an inpatient at Capri Hospital arguing with my clinician about how this was all my bloody fault.

I know now how good psychologists are supposed to treat people just like me, so I believe Brent (my psychologist) graced me with a certain period of time to burn myself out with the "I could have," "I should have." Then he picked up a marker and drew a diagram on a board and stood back and explained how the mechanics of my brain worked. I sat there opening and closing my mouth like a fish, and then came out with: "It can't be that bloody simple." His answer, "Denise you have a wonderful ability to overcomplicate simple matters. Here's what is happening inside of your head."

As the time in that bubble passed by, I learned more and more about the psychology of addiction, morning and afternoon classes run by the majority of professionals who had come from addiction, or if not, they had been touched or impacted by it enough to seek to make it their career to help those that suffered from it.

We learned how it happens, why it happens, and how we can grow stronger with every passing day that we all gratefully counted since we had chosen to stop. The private therapy with a clinician three times a week helped to layout a personal road map with reasons for how I got here. Here I learned that I was slapping a big fat Band-Aid on seeping wounds of underlying issues that I had never dealt with. My Band-Aid brand was alcohol, but the make and model of band-aid others use doesn't matter. It can be gambling, sex addiction, social media addiction, shopping, even CD collecting. They are all the same, they will all take and take until there is no more, and they will all do the same thing to that machine in your head.

# CHAPTER 25

# *Bright Lights and Dark Places*

My 28 days in that bubble called a Mental Health and Addiction Hospital was the setting of a stage for a turning point in my life.

There were so many individual professionals helping me make my way forward, helping me break down and understand how I got here and helping me learn how to continue to go forth towards the life I wanted while I started to uncover my real identity—what were the bones of me. I say the bones of me because I knew what I was in my heart and in my soul and saw my bones as the big Daddy that combined all these elements to complete me.

I know I was born someone uniquely me, and that social and economic environments would influence my personality. The genes of generations flowed through me, but I saw this more in my physical appearance with my father's forefathers coming from Spain, washing up on the shores of Ireland over the time of the Spanish Armada. I have dark Irish eyes and olive skin. I carry a surname like Cloughley that only a country of people that I have never visited can correctly pronounce and spell.

When I did speak up, which in the beginning wasn't a lot, I would try and turn their scientific evidence-based knowledge around mental health and addiction into an open forum which consisted of my continuous statements that I wasn't strong enough to stop it, and that I showed weakness and caved into an easy way out.

I'm going to leave the psychological scientific evidence-based information stuff that has been studied and acknowledged worldwide for years up to Dr. Gavin Jones who writes the conclusion to this book. It's his field that he has spent the last 20 years working in, and it's his knowledge coupled with raw passion and compassion that has helped give thousands of people around the world the knowledge and tools to live the fullest of lives that they were born to own.

I credit two other people with shining a very bright light for me on my path forward. While Michelle had thrown me a tiny step ladder with the phone conversation to get me here, these two men pulled back the blinds covering my eyes. They removed the cotton wool from my ears and shoved it firmly in my mouth.

Between a group facilitator named Aston who was a - no holds barred, don't argue with me - recovering methamphetamine addict, and Brent who was also amongst other things a dealer who had been a guest of her majesty's facility for a long while, before turning his life around and then turning his life into getting degrees before turning his life into helping others that made me shut up, sit up, and listen.

I heard words I understood. I started to understand how addiction to a substance happens. It was simply explained, so I found it simple to understand and accept. Really if you break it all down, it's quite simple.

I know this much is true because it's what I held on to in those early years, then later repeated to so many hundreds of people to give them just a slight insight into how they possibly got to where they found themselves. Those suffering addictions and those standing in the shadows praying for help while watching the person they love disappear into a bottle or pipe.

## Dopamine (hormone and neurotransmitter)

Addiction is a complex brain disorder that doesn't have one single, obvious cause. It's been proven that Dopamine, a neurotransmitter plays a part; still a small piece in the puzzle, but it plays a role. Dopamine is known as a "pleasure chemical." Think of the term Dopamine rush. We all have it, and we all get it. For example, winning the Lotto would produce one big mind spinning rush of Dopamine. However, it's transmitted in small ways as well. When you see someone you love who has been absent for a long time. Hell, a coffee, if it's your go-to, will give you a dopamine kick, though it's more when you're ordering a coffee, not so much the drinking of it.

A new purchase (not the receiving but the finding and buying part), finding a $100 note on the ground, purchasing that bottle of Sav to salute to the end of a hard day, walking up the path to your dealers... Boom, little mini dopamine feel-good explosions everywhere.

Experiences that make you feel good activate your brain's reward center, which responds by releasing dopamine. The reward centre is also intricately linked to memory and motivation. This release of dopamine causes your brain to focus more of its attention on the experience. As a result, you're left with a strong memory of the pleasure you felt. This strong memory can prompt you to make more of an effort to experience it again and again, seeking out certain experiences to continue to make you feel good.

So, to break down dopamine, he has a whistle from Mr. and Mrs. reward, memory, and motivation centers that something good is about to happen, and that they did their job in remembering. He then motivates and lets the person know that more of that particular feel good is coming. Dopamine fires up to do his job, to combine all the family together and give the owner a rush of pleasure.

Alcohol and drugs seriously make little ol' dopamine work hard. Chemically addictive substances themselves have done a good job of telling our family of memories and rewards that this is good, so motivation is telling you to go and get more. Eventually making dopamine work harder to release more and more neurotransmitters.

The more we seek and source to activate this hard-working neurotransmitter that we most probably didn't even know lives in our heads, the more overworked and a bit tired it becomes trying to make you have a rush of feel goods. So, as us humans do, if externally what we are doing to get what we think is giving us the rush, and it's not doing what it used to do in small doses, we up it. We know it made us feel good, happier, calmer, brighter, and better before. All it needs is a little more to take us right back to feeling chipper. The only problem is that we never do just a little more.

While it's actually the magic juices and complex bits of what's already within our brains working hard together to make us feel good, the popping in the body immediately starts working hard against this tight-knit family, confusing the shit out of everyone who lives in there.

Below is information from the Hazelden Betty Ford manuals.

Alcohol has a profound effect on the complex structures of the brain. It blocks chemical signals between brain cells (called neurons), leading to the common immediate symptoms of intoxication, including impulsive behavior, slurred speech, poor memory, and slowed reflexes. If heavy drinking continues over a long period of time, the brain adapts to the blocked signals by responding more dramatically to certain brain chemicals (called neurotransmitters). After alcohol leaves the system, the brain continues over activating the neurotransmitters, causing painful and potentially dangerous withdrawal symptoms that can damage brain cells. This damage is made worse by drinking binges and sudden withdrawal. Alcohol's damage to the brain can take several forms. The first is neurotoxicity, which occurs when neurons overreact to neurotransmitters for too long. Too much exposure to a neurotransmitter can cause neurons to eventually "burn out." Since neurons make up the pathways between different parts of the brain, when they begin burning out, it can cause a noticeable slowing in the reactions of these pathways. In addition to pathway damage, brain matter itself is also damaged by heavy alcohol use. People with alcohol dependence often experience "brain shrinkage," which is a reduced volume of both gray matter (cell bodies) and white matter (cell pathways) over time. There are some subtle differences in how brain damage occurs in men and women, but regardless of gender, loss of brain matter increases with age and amount of alcohol consumed.

And for Methamphetamine, you most certainly don't get off lightly either:

Users of crystal meth report initially feeling euphoric, experiencing an intense, long-lasting rush after the first use. This is because methamphetamine floods the brain with dopamine, the "feel-good" chemical responsible for pleasure, reward, and motivation. Blood pressure spikes, thoughts race, and users often have to keep moving even though they're accomplishing nothing. "While under the influence of meth, users can have the illusion of being more powerful and productive than usual, and then they actually are. Although this can feel good for the meth user, it can cause real problems. Meth can make people feel more socially outgoing, talkative, and self-confident. But equally, they can behave bizarrely and become distant from positive social relationships, and not realize they may appear ridiculous to others," explains Elizabeth Hartney, PhD., in *Very Well Mind*.

After the rush comes the high. If snorting the drug in crystal form, the high will come on in three to five minutes; if swallowing methamphetamine, it can take 15 to 20 minutes. The length of time the drug stays in your system depends on how much was used, your age (as you get older, your body has a slower metabolism, and it can take longer to eliminate toxins), and your health (if you're unhealthy, it will take longer for your body to get rid of substances). The drug's effects can last anywhere from six to12 hours, which can lead people to continue using it to keep the high going. Users who binge on crystal meth can stay awake for as long as 10 days, often subsisting with very little food or drink.

"Tweaking" occurs when the body and mind of the meth addict stop reacting to the drug, and the addict "enters a state that is almost psychotic," according to *Methamphetamine Addiction.*

"Tweakers" can be unpredictable, with the user experiencing hallucinations; paranoia; and picking, scraping, or digging at the face or skin, either due to breakouts or because they feel phantom bugs crawling on or under the skin's surface ("ice bugs" or "meth sores"). This crawling feeling is due to an increased body temperature, leading to sweating and oily skin, combined with the fact that the body is dehydrated.

The stimulant can also bring about a severe crash when the inebriating effects wear off, causing the user to sleep for days afterward.

Common physical effects of "coming down" from the drug use include body aches, heartburn, and feeling extremely lethargic, nauseous, and confused. When meth wears off, dopamine and serotonin are both depleted, resulting in anxiety and depression.

Meth addiction is a vicious cycle. Once you develop a tolerance to the drug, it takes more and more methamphetamine to achieve the same stimulating effect. A second consequence is that when the high is over, the user feels a corresponding low or depression as a result of a depleted supply of dopamine. Users are well aware that such feelings can quickly be countered by another dose. While the depths of this low tend to correspond to the heights of the user's high, the long-term reduction in dopamine levels for people with meth addiction leads to anhedonia, the inability to experience pleasure from simple, everyday things.

Simply put, you're taking something like alcohol or drugs to seek a good time in the beginning. In my case, it was alcohol. It made me happy, it relaxed me. Many people celebrate and commiserate with alcohol. In a lot of situations today, I'm faced with it. If you don't drink, you're looked upon by others as if something is wrong with you. Why? There must be a reason for that.

The more it made me happy, the more my brain registered that I was feeling good, sending me signals to continue to seek rewards. The more I did this, the more certain areas of my brain had to work to keep up with it all. Memory, motivation, and rewards were telling me to keep going. The more I drank, the more I needed to get the same effect. The more I drank, that lower bit under my head started to suffer, and the organ department didn't like it all at first, but sadly sugars and toxins and chemicals in the alcohol were also making my organs reliant, so much so that they all reacted negatively and painfully when I'd suddenly shut up the shop. The withdrawals are painful and confusing for all the departments of our body and mind, even the early stages that everyone experiences, like the shakes, headaches, and feeling sick. Everyone has heard of the hair of the dog saying, so you open up the shop again and repeat it.

Your entire body is so confused. Your mind that has now become very unwell is telling you how much you need this. And your organs, although rejecting it also, join the unwell party and send signals of two kinds. Despair, here we go again, and then the relief that your body is getting the sugars and chemicals washing around again.

It's just a vicious cycle that, if not recognized early enough, will continue till it physically owns you. Parts of your mind are still well, but by now very confused. If you suffer from any kind of issues surrounding your mental health, no matter what it is, relieving it with depressants such as alcohol and meth will only make matters worse. You do not know this of course, because you are just having that drink, smoke, pipe, sniff, or pill, because once upon a time, it made you feel good, and your memory and reward system is going to make sure you never forget that.

Do you need to get to where I did before you can stop this? No! Do you need a rock bottom? No! Michelle melted me when she once said:

> *Denise, it's not your fault that you arrived*
> *at the gates of addiction, but it is all on*
> *you now that you know you are there.*

I knew it was only the beginning of the end when I arrived at the bubble on the 6th of March 2014. When day 24 came around, and I really needed to decide what was next, I started to get really scared. My health was slowly returning, my hair had started to sprout, my nails were growing, my skin had a glow, my teeth, well I had to spend money fixing them quickly. I wanted to smile, and I actually felt like smiling. In fact, I'd even started having little belly laughs, something that was a weird feeling for me. My mind and my organs were working together again to overcome the state of trauma that they had been living in for years. By now I was clued up about how to feed all the important parts of me, not only food and water, but how to care for my body, mind, and soul.

I had an exceedingly long way to go and I knew it. I didn't want to go back to Wellington, but my "mother heart" was heavy with the absence of Jackson. I just wanted to go home and fix things with him—for him. The damage I had done was really beginning to sink in as the days were growing longer between me and the bottle.

I was hearing, 'just one day at a time, Denise. Just one day at a time'. I can tell you, somedays it was a blink at a time. Then it morphed into minutes, hours, and then… Yes! I learned to just do what I could for today—wake up sober, go to bed sober, one step at a time, and tomorrow repeat it. So, I did.

Capri Hospital had an outpatient group that was run every day from 10 am till 11 am when all the old clients would come in and gather around in a group facilitated mostly by Aston. I envied this bunch of bubbly, bouncy people walking in every morning, having their own huddle, with each person given the opportunity to proudly call out their fiercely important and proud stats.

*"Hi, I'm Luke, alcoholic, 77 days sober today."*

I'd wonder why they were counting. Then the deeper question rose: why are you all so happy? In time, I'd learn why.

Counting was important, because the further you got away from your substance, the harder it would try and crawl back to you. A small voice would start banging on in my ear saying, "We weren't that bad together—you and I." I replied:

*Let's think about that. I totalled just about*
*every relationship with anyone that mattered*
*to me, I've deeply hurt everyone I love, I was*
*98% dead when I finally got it that you weren't*
*my fucking friend, and now I'm thinking*
*about getting back on the road with you?*

Counting the days bloody mattered. Sometimes, that number was the only thing that stopped me on some tough days. That number stopped me from getting back in the driver's seat of a car that was heading directly for a cliff.

A few days before, I was still insanely thinking I'd go back to Wellington. Brent came to me and said, "I don't want you to return to Wellington yet. I want you to consider staying here in Auckland and coming to the OP group daily. Just like a job. You have to make this a job, Denise. Learning to live your life sober is going to take time and you need to work on that. You need aftercare support, and you have it here."

I decided to stay nearby in a motel for a week or so and come in every day. But Brent had different ideas on how he was going to make sure I wasn't another sad statistic, so he hunted around for a sober house for me. On the eve of day 27, he came to me with an offer of a place for me to stay with people I knew, liked, and trusted; others just like me. So just like that, on day 28, I left the bubble that had shown me what hope looks like and I moved in with Mel and Brendon for not one week or two, but for the next 547 days of life after the bottle.

## CHAPTER 26

# *HALTS*

I did as I chose, not as I was told. I went to OP every single day, only for an hour, but my day revolved around it. I surrounded myself with my fellow sober travellers and listened to how they were overcoming things at 60, 90, and 120 days. I had a fair idea of what obstacles were going to be coming towards me. Go early, leave early to any function that might have your substance at it, or, better still, don't go at all. Start to slowly make amends, but only do it when you mean it. You don't get points for how many I'm sorrys you hand out every week.

Follow **HALTS**. I lived by this one when I felt I was on shaky ground. Halt, stop and break down what you are feeling. Hungry? Eat. Angry? Seek someone safe to vent to. Lonely? Seek connection. Tired? Sleep. Stressed? Go to your personal plan to alleviate it. Everyone should do this when their world is starting to spin out of control.

It was a big job, this art of staying sober stuff, harder than I'd ever imagined, but every day I got up and just did it. And every night I fell into bed and thanked whoever my guardian angel was for watching over me, for not packing it in and going into early retirement, for keeping me here, and for allowing me to slowly finally start to understand how I'd arrived here.

I questioned Aston once about this dopamine happy juice, asking if there was any way I could make this dopamine happy juice produce itself any quicker. He just looked at me for a bit then said, "Do you think happiness is just going to come to you, Denise? Do you think you just sit and wait for happiness to come knocking at your door? You need to get up, get out there, and look for things to make you happy. Then, yes, dopamine will slowly start being produced more quickly again. All those important parts will start doing a little more than a half-decent job." So, I did.

The idea of trying to follow the leader or be anything but myself never occurred to me. It annoyed people I know. At the OP group, I'd say:

*Hi, Denise, 29 days, and I'm a gratefully
retired connoisseur of fine wines.*

I know it pissed people off, but I had been called an alcoholic for years now, and it wasn't my handle anymore. I knew I was one. Enough already! I did not want to remind myself over and over verbally. My thoughts and voices inside my head did enough of that for me.

I tried it on once at an AA meeting, and it went down like a lead balloon. A close second was when I was asked to share, and I said I really enjoyed AA and that it was about the only place I was going to meet my new ex-husband. Don't get me wrong, AA was part of my early recovery. I just sometimes felt this need to break out from telling my sad sack war story. So, I try to lighten the moment. I still go to meetings now and again when I'm in a faraway city on my own, or when I just want to surround myself with people seeking help and hearing stories of others just like me who dared to face up and surround themselves in support and help for a better life than the bottle offered.

I didn't really conform in many ways. I decided I'd try and get those happy juices flowing by becoming a personal stylist for women. This was easy. I'd go op-shopping every single day on the bus all over the entire Auckland District. I'd buy good clothes with good labels, take them home, wash them, present them on a mannequin I called Willamina, and then list them on Trade Me.

As women started to buy a certain size and a certain style, I'd go shopping for similar clothes. It worked. I had a great following. For one of my clients, I would send her a photo from the shop, and she would say yes or no. She never knew she was helping me stay sober by allowing me to shop for her, and she was letting me continue to make my happy come back to me faster.

Every day, for the best part of 14 months, I did this. Then, a bit like Forrest Gump, I suddenly stopped and thought, I'm done with this now. I turned around to see what was next. Just as well, because right about then, Trade me started sending me emails asking if I was trading commercially.

I also decided I was going to brighten my world by wearing unimaginable combinations of outrageously bright colors smashed together. I found looking at bright orange and lime green made me so happy when I looked in the mirror. Brendon, my flat mate, commented at one point that I looked like a Unicorn had shat all over me. What it did though was make other people smile at me. Everyone smiled as they walked towards me and, in return, made me smile back. My explosion of Unicorn shat on my wardrobe years was so much fun for everyone that one time when I turned up for a function in black, everyone asked me what the hell was wrong.

At 60 days, I thought thank God I made it here. At 90, I thought maybe I'll do another 90. But I made myself a promise: if I'm not ok by the time I get to a year, I would look at my choices. By the time I got to 10 months, I had all but forgotten that promise. By the time 365 days came around, I knew that for this day, this week, this month, and for the next years of my life, there's no bloody way I am ever going back to that hell of a life I lived while in active addiction. Still, I kept it at one day at a time.

It was an uphill climb, and then just one day, it really wasn't so hard anymore. Little by little, I started to notice things around me like the amazing color of the lemon tree outside my door, smells, senses, feeling that there was beauty in front of me, around me, and in me. I knew that I could make this as easy or as hard as I liked. Either way, it couldn't change the outcome. I was never going back. So, I chose easy.

They say you should search for a higher power, and I understand that. My power to start with was to just say no more, to sit with myself, and to know that I could do this. I could live the one life I have without relying on a substance to show me happiness. I did then and I still do now get up by 5:30 am and watch the daybreak. Then at dusk, I sit there and watch the day close. I thank the power in me and the power of love and connection for giving me this moment, this day, this life.

As I started to understand me better, the things within me that led me towards seeking escape and detachment from reality and clarity, through good guidance, care, and compassionate support, I was able to start making my way slowly towards a life I was truly destined to live. I believe that what is truly meant for you in this world will never pass you by.

When I first started pouring myself a glass of life instead of drinking myself to death, I only had one thought: to ease the darkness that I had been covering others in for so long. As I started to uncover how I got here, and as I started to understand what Substance Use Disorder was, so did my family. They were also seeking and learning along the way. My parents were and still are my greatest supporters, especially my mother who is now advocating for people like me, telling people to educate themselves around what addiction is, so they can have a clearer understanding and acceptance that alcoholism is a disease, not a choice. We were returning to each other the further I put the distance between myself and alcohol.

My parents agreed to come to an AA meeting with me while we were together in Dunedin one time. We sat and listened to the meeting. Afterward, a lovely lady about Mum's age came up to us. She had recognized Mum from their swimming group. She introduced herself to me, and said to my Mum, "Pat, I'd never guessed you had an alcohol issue just like me." They have become good friends ever since that day, and my mother, who wasn't a big drinker anyway, joined me and quit for good.

It cost me $25,000 to save my life, about the same as it would have cost to tidy up my affairs and bury me. Id assigned Joel as a trustee of my investments. By now he was in Thailand. I still don't how he was contacted and how he arranged payment. But the important thing was that he did make the payment, and with this, telling me that he knew I was there, and I felt some calm knowing that he could at least enjoy Thailand, without thinking a phone call was coming about me.

It took baby steps to rebuild my relationship with my beautiful darling boy Joel. He loved me deeply. Trusting me? That took a lot longer. He was counting the days as was I. I didn't know this until one day he phoned and said, "Mum, you're 100 days today. Do you know what that means to me, Mum? I'm not holding my breath anymore."

Jack was the baby boy that I left behind at twelve years young. Three long years is an awfully long time for a young teenage boy growing up with a mostly absent mother. My little rocket pocket, he was fifteen years old when his mother finally permanently reentered his life to mother him into adulthood. And this I did. We spent long weekends and all the holidays until he eventually finished school and moved to Auckland to live full-time with me.

As I started to forgive myself, my children also started to forgive their mother. My life is complete and whole with my children in it, but it's the bones of me, it's Denise, who saw this through to the place I am in my life today. It may have been my love for those who loved me that got me to stand up, step up, and take a chance. But I had to want it for me the most in the end to have any hope of making it happen.

# CHAPTER 27

# *New, new beginnings*

I returned from Australia and Joel's 30th birthday in June 2015, 16 months since I finished drinking poison out of bottles. I needed more in my world for a while now, but I'd been self-employed since the late 1980s, so finding a job wasn't that easy.

I had become a little less unemployable in jobs that I would have liked as I turned 50 in March and celebrated by returning home to my mountains and my southern Lakes. My friend Karen did a beautiful job of arranging a gathering with twelve good, true, old girlfriends who knew me well. We enjoyed a long lunch at the Bathhouse, a restaurant on the shores of the lake in Queenstown that she still owns. I blew that bloody white elephant right out of the room that day I turned 50 by choosing to supply all my favorite wines for the girls to enjoy. I merrily joined in as loud and happy as the next one, me with my lemon, lime, and bitters—my going out drink of the time.

I had been doing a huge amount of volunteering at Capri hospital, amongst other things. I was running the newbies group. Those new in every week would gather on a Wednesday night, and together talk of their fears, while I listened and reassured them that they were in the right place. They just needed to have courage, and everything would be alright. I really wanted to start looking at how I could combine my communication skills and my journey so far to help others that were struggling.

The CEO of Capri Hospital, Dale, overheard me talking to another outpatient about how I was going for an interview the next day for a job I didn't really want, but that would be better than doing a lot of nothing like I was right now.

I went home that night to a phone call from Dale asking if I would be interested in coming into the offices at Capri the next day for a job interview. I didn't need music to dance that night. I was bouncing around like I was at a rock festival.

17 months after I called Michelle on the 5th of March 2014, I started working beside her learning the business of offering people without hope the hope they needed to believe that change was possible if they were willing to chance it.

I almost didn't have a job two weeks later as Dale just couldn't get me to conform to the way Michelle did things. Finally, Michelle said, "Let Denise do it her way. She's unique and she can't pretend she's anybody she's not." Damn straight, Michelle! The next day, I had my first shot of doing things my way. The very first person who phoned, thanked me for understanding him. He was admitted a few days later.

I never looked back. And nor did Dale. The board filled up with new admissions as did the arrivals lounge.

*Welcome to your new life where I greet the newbies*
*with a massive hug, and the words, "It's ok, you're*
*here now. We are going to take care of you."*

Inside of me was burning a bright torch of hope, a torch that I would carry for every one of those beautiful brave souls who let me convince them that they were worthy of a chance to have a better life. We offered them the path to a life where they could learn to understand and be validated on how their underlying issues had led them to self-medicate on a substance that was no longer their friend. I knew where they had come from, and I knew where they were going. All they had to do was find some hope, then believe they could.

Hundreds and hundreds of people made it. I know this because I've kept in touch with so many of them over the years. They can call me up now and ask, "Do you remember me?" I answer, "Absolutely! I can even remember the name of your dog!"

Sometimes at Capri, Brent, who was now also my boss, or Michelle or Dale would make the mistake of asking me to take over a group if a clinician was busy. The procedure was to put the video on that they were scheduled to watch. But I, little Miss Individuality, had much bigger plans for turning that hour into a discussion time about no longer pussyfooting around the minor stuff, and getting real.

The clients liked the change of pace, and as they would turn over sometimes every 28 days, some who had extended would tell the newer clients, and they started requesting the "Denise shut up, sit up show." My favorite subject was about letting go of your minor crap. An example of this was one older man with an English accent who was very proper and so much fun. I used to overhear him several times saying he could do this, he wanted this. But he knew when that clock on the wall at home in his kitchen hit 3 pm on the dot, he was going to struggle. The opportunity arose, and I had the joy of taking a group. So, I went in there, and I opened the subject up on what they felt their smaller struggles were going to be. I asked him and he answered me. He talked about how it would be tough when the clock on the wall hit 3 o'clock. So, I told him I had a simple answer for that, and I handed him a little hammer. Here you go! Take that home, and smash that fucking clock. Problem Fixed.

Sometimes there are remarkably simple answers to overly complicated matters.

I was scheduled to facilitate the startup group one morning. It was an early 8 am wake up, smell the coffee, and let's get on with the day group. Guy used to run these as the owner and a recovered alcoholic. He was interesting to listen to—a no bullshit kind of man who would make you lean forward with interest in what he was saying. He ran his own little thing called Radio Capri when he would call up old clients and ask them how they were doing, allowing the clients in treatment to ask questions around how they coped with certain issues that may have presented itself to the recovering client.

At the time we had a large number of women who were all mostly mothers. A lot of their children were around Joel's age group, so I thought I would arrange to call Joel in Aussie, and he could tell them what it was like for him, then and now. To give them some hope that their children would forgive them, and their relationships would be restored. I handed it over to Joel. I'd been two-plus years sober by now, so I didn't expect to hear the words Joel spoke. He told them that he had lived a life of hell over the final years of my addiction. He talked about how he had lived in a state of constant anxiety that was not part of his make-up. He recounted the times that he paced the floor for hours after my early morning calls panicking about what to do, that it affected his relationships, his work, and his life so greatly that loving me was unconditional, but living with it was not. Then he said that the greatest gift he would ever receive in his life was my sobriety.

I know for a fact that not one of the women in that group that morning returned to the life they'd had the courage to leave. I know them, I know their sons and daughters, and I know Joel's words were a beautiful gift to their mending "mother hearts."

I was given the chance to attend courses and learn more about the backbone of mental health and addiction. My compassion for others along with my growing knowledge of the ways the mind worked enthralled me. My work was my work; however, my own sobriety and recovery were for my own time. I was told this when I was first employed there, so I started to learn the most helpful skill that I'm gifted with today. Compartmentalization. Put work into a compartment for when you're at work, and don't take it home; home is for peace, and calm, and contentment. I had to remember to take time for me—time for growing into the person I'd always known that was there, tucked away deep inside my head.

Oh my, I had so much joy in my life doing what I was doing, living the way I was choosing. My work was so fulfilling as was my own time. I'd become close friends with the mother of a guy that I was in treatment with, thinking when I first met her that she was his sister. Maggie was my friend and my rock through some hard times, and was responsible for many years filled with laughter.

> *I know I would have gotten through those early*
> *Auckland years Maggie, but having you in*
> *them walking alongside me, both of us sharing*
> *and caring and growing young into our 50s*
> *are memories that I will treasure forever. I've*
> *never told you this, but thank you for being*
> *exactly who you are, and for being my friend.*

They say you never get over an addiction—it's always lurking there in the far reaches of your mind, and I have an extremely healthy, clear, and present respect for that. But I don't refer to myself as a recovering alcoholic. Nope, that's not for me. If I'm recovering, it means I'm still sick. Yes, I'm one drink away from that doorstep at that nice man's house trying desperately to stop shaking enough to get the poison down my throat. I'm one drink away from Dead. But I don't avoid alcohol—not way back then in 2014 and not now. I'll drag my friends around a liquor store telling them to buy this wine or that. To try that flavour of gin and give me a full report of the taste.

If I wanted to fit in this world where alcohol is everywhere you look, then I knew I had to learn to live with it. Imagine how many functions, birthdays, or events I couldn't go to if I couldn't be around it. I'd be a sad sack Doris with no friends. That's not my personality. So, a secret that I taught myself incredibly early on is to take myself down that old road, the run with all the signposts pointing to a cliff. I would mentally go to the supermarket and buy the wine, get home, hide it, then drink it, lose all my clarity and my senses, throw up, and then fall into a comatose sleep. I'd wake up not knowing what I did the night before, throw up again, and repeat. I also mentally tasted the alcohol, which in the end tasted like vinegar and went down my throat like poison.

It worked for me then. Now alcohol is far, far away, in another lifetime, lived long ago. It's a memory scar. Yes, I'm one drink away. I'm an alcoholic, but that's 5% of what makes me, me. The other

95% of me is many things. I'm far from perfect. I most certainly know that. I have annoying habits. But I'm me. I know what I want, and I know what I don't.

What I know with absolute certainty is that it's ok not to be ok in your world.

If you're not ok, look around you, reach out, because out there somewhere, is love. Out there somewhere is connection. Out there is help. Out there, there is someone to take your hand and shine a torch very brightly on a path to show the way. You just have to say you want it, stand up, and step up, onto that tiny ladder towards that tiny light to start finding a tiny way forwards to who you are truly meant to be.

# CHAPTER 28

# *Seeking Solace*

I was in one of the best places in my life by mid-2016 both mentally and physically. My organs had survived the war zone era where I had gravely assaulted them all day and every day for years. However, mentally is where it all really counts. I saw my life change, and becoming psychologically strong was the game-changer. I learned that holding on to things that had happened in my life was clouding my ability to move forward with clarity. The blame game can play a big part in holding people back.

I was great at the blame game, and, at times, it was 100% someone else's fault, particularly events that impacted me greatly in my life that had been out of my control. I learned that holding on to them was like me continuing to drink poison while hoping that person who had hurt me would die. The events had happened long ago, but I was still living with them at the forefront of my memory every day.

I learned with professional help to talk about them, have my hurt and confusion validated, process what happened, then decide whether someone else's actions that hurt me so dearly demanded a presence in my life today. They didn't; it was only continuing to hurt me psychologically when that person had either long ago moved on or was dead. So, who was suffering? I was. There are books out there about letting go, but the one true way I was able to do this was to become clockwise. My father had owned a yacht he named clough-wise, so this seemed an appropriate name for my technique.

Two major issues that are mine alone led me to feel unworthy, among other things that contributed greatly to the lack of my self-confidence along with my inability to feel good about myself. So, I set the clock for a certain time of the day, normally around the time I understood all the good juices in my head were aligned for clarity, and I'd allow myself 1 hour to think about it. Process what I could have done; how could I have changed it? all those thoughts that were individual to me. Then when that hour was up, I told myself repeatedly, "I can't change my past. I can only change my future." Then I reduced this exercise to 45 minutes, then 30, until one day, I just stopped. I thought about how I had lived in my head, in my memory for so long. I spoke to my blame and pain, "Let go of what you don't own, and forgive yourself."

*I don't want you there anymore, I'm so tired*
*of you taking up space in my thoughts and*
*the time the clock has given you every day.*

I wrote something really nasty down on paper, and I went down to the back of the property, and I buried those memories. They no longer belonged in my head, holding me back. Now they lie in a hole, at a house that I left long ago. Of course, thoughts will still enter my head, but I can no longer align the memory of those events with me. They are in a hole that I dug in the dirt, deep in the ground, right where they belong.

The CEO, Dale, called a meeting of all the staff of Capri Hospital in the spring of 2016. We were given a notification of a proposal to close for good. It had been 17 years of the Smith family owning and working this operation, and for reasons that respectfully are known only to them, they had decided that the time had come to shut down.

Everyone was devastated, but for me personally, it signaled an end to the burning flame I was carrying so brightly inside of me. It was allowing me to have a way and a means to shine a light on a path of hope for change for the ever-increasing number of people out there suffering from mental health/addiction.

I had a gift to be able to differentiate and move freely verbally between the people who were calling Capri. I could tell from their voices, from their account of their struggle with their mental health, and the type of substance they were using, which was the best way to connect with them. Slowly, softly to begin with, and no matter what, it normally ended with me hitting them hard between the eyeballs with the facts of where this was all going to lead for them if they didn't take the lifeline I was throwing them. Always with compassion, always with understanding, and always with the undeniable simple scientific facts that were undebatable.

I'd become a chameleon that could change my color to blend into anyone's background. Again compartmentalization had truly become my new middle name, and as soon as I hung up from one person, I could leave their notes in a secure file; one on the computer and one in my head, and move on to the next person.

Four years after Capri closed, I still recall so many of the most enlightening moments. I saw people who had arrived broken and lost slowly start to mend, physically at first, then everyday small changes appeared. To hear them belly laugh and surprise themselves that they could feel joy again. To see the light return to their eyes, and to see their families become part of this new journey. To see life refreshed. To have been a part of all that fills me with such gladness.

*I'll never forget any of you. Thank you for keeping in contact with me, thank you for showing me that being able to help you then, gave me the "want to" to continue on the path that I walk now.*

We had 4 weeks to find new jobs. Again, I was back in a place where my age and my employment record did not reflect enough to secure interviews. Self-employment is a wonderful thing, but it is hard to align working in the film industry with trying to get a job at a Doctor's surgery as a receptionist. My earlier years in communications and working in a supervisory position of emergency services in telephone exchanges didn't amount to anything when applying for jobs with roles in emergency services with the police. I had 2 DICs and that was a mark against me. I'd only recently applied and gone through the process of getting my license back three years after I was eligible to. I could apply for jobs in other rehabs, but as these are government departments, generally speaking, you need a certificate in education rather than a PhD. in Alcoholism that I had gained.

Then it came to me. Why not carry on doing exactly what I've been doing, but my way? So, I looked further into it.

I had the support of those that I held in the highest regard who worked with me at Capri.  But that's where it stopped, and I was on my own. What I wanted to do was unprecedented, unique, and anybody's guess as to where it was going to lead.

I got in touch and was contacted by two incredibly special people to me, Mark Quickfall and Jenni Mc Bride—two people who I'd see create and make their lives what they were, with where they had come from, and the courage and belief in themselves as to where they were today.

Mark had been my flat mate when I was 16, my boss when I was 17, my introduction to Greg when I was 18, and our best man when I was 19. He, along with his wonderful bubbly and beautiful wife Jackie, made success after success of companies that he had started or taken over. He knew his stuff when it came to business, and so I asked him to look at mine, and give his honest educated opinion on whether this concept could work. He was in Korea at the time, but Jackie had passed on a message that I had rung. Bless that man, he called from there to make sure everything was ok. He finally looked the concept over and answered me with this.

*"It's a good idea, Denise. It has the potential*
*to work, but, overall, why I think it will work*
*is because of the deep driven passion you have*
*to help those that were just like you. That's*
*what you need and that's enough to try."*

When Jenni Mc Bride contacted me, I was expecting to struggle financially to set this up and thought it was going to take a long time to earn any sort of decent income. She heard what I was thinking of doing through Karen and called me. Jenni was the maternity nurse, working in the tiny maternity home in Queenstown when Joel was born. I knew Jenni before this but not as well as I got to know her later.

The day Greg and I left the maternity home on the 30th of May 1985 with our 7-day old baby Joel, we gathered in the nursery with Jenni and took photos of us all—not intentionally, but we were standing under a clock. It said 2 pm. By 3:30 pm, Jenni was involved in a horrific car accident - which was no fault of her own - that stole her eyesight. Joel was the last baby she saw, and to this day she can still describe him in detail.

Jenni is a warrior of astronomical nature. She never let her blindness hold her back.  For 35 years now she's skied, water skied, and ran New York marathons, letting nothing hold her back. Under all of that, she's Jenni, a really beautiful soul who phoned me to say, "I believe in you, Denise. I know you can make this happen, and I want to offer you financial help." So, she did. Jenni didn't want any ownership or recognition in Seeking Solace, but over the years I've told her parts of what her faith in me has done. Without naming names of people's lives that she played a role in changing, she's been instrumental in directing one particular mother to me, who in turn was able to reach out for help with her daughter's need for Solace. These days, both mother and daughter live a calm and content life.

I've never really told anyone who was behind me making the final decision to do what I do today. My family and friends believed I could and wholly supported me, but it was Mark and Jenni's faith in me that finally convinced me that I could do this.

I did a lot of hours reading the ins and outs of what was required to start my own company. In the end, it was that strong burning desire to not put down that Olympic size torch that burned within, to not stop what I knew I was capable of doing, that lead me to my final decision to officially launch my own company once more. Seeking Solace was born. Solace, help in times of great despair, seeking because thousands and thousands of souls out there were looking for a way out of their entrapment to a substance and the fragmentation of what they didn't understand was happening in their head.

They say most people who suffer from Substance Use Disorder have remarkably high IQs.  If the clientele I was dealing with had anything to go on, it highly reflected this fact. I'm in no way trying to box this. I'm the last person to discriminate between social, economic, racial, or religious differences. But the fact of the matter was that those who had come to Capri Hospital had a way and a means to afford the private treatment. Among many of the clients were judges, lawyers, professors, CEOs, doctors, nurses, police, and emergency services personal. They were the people who went under the radar for so long because they could. They presented well, spoke well, lived in nice houses, and their children went to nice schools.

They were the highly functioning category that didn't appear in the courts or the parks or in the hospitals. They had the finances and social status to cover their tracks and cover them for an exceptionally long time. They are the unnoticed numbers, so when the wheels did finally come off and they fell off that cliff, it was often a fast, rapid, ugly fall from grace.

This was my target audience - the ones who went unnoticed until it was too late. Their marriages and their careers were over in one fell swoop. Along with their struggling mental and physical health states, many didn't make it to a phone to call for help or reach up to be picked up. A lot left a note of goodbye instead.

As I stated, addiction doesn't give a fuck who you are, or what your postcode is. It doesn't care if you wear Jimmy Choo's or Jandals, and it doesn't give a toss if it's riding along in the body of someone who is driving a 2020 model car. You are all heading in the same direction, on a road to hell. Our bodies and our brains are all made of the same grey matter and the same organs. Mental health will present itself in all the different forms; anxiety, depression, grief, and trauma, to name a few. It's our brain's chemistry that all works to the beat of the same drum when you add an addictive substance to mix.

C H A P T E R  29

# *Seeking Solace is born*

Capri Hospital closed on the 16th of September 2016, and by the 21st of September 2016, Seeking Solace was in business with its first client, and I've never looked back.

I was navigating a woman who worked in the police force for years and who clearly needed to stay under the radar, although she had already been stood down from work. She so wanted to get help, but confidential care and good treatment in a not so public place was a high priority.

I'd already done a huge amount of research on other rehabs that offered a similar structure to Capri's psychological evidence-based treatment, with professional psychiatrists, psychologists, and psychotherapists. Along with understanding what addiction is, you need to understand and breakdown how you got there. These two things were like a partnership/marriage of great significance. One didn't work without the other.

I had full knowledge of what was in New Zealand, so I started to widen the scope and search further afield. I spoke for hours with the owner of rehab in Melbourne as well as a sister treatment clinic she owned on the Gold Coast of Australia.

She was very much like me. She knew that if you want something to work, get your big girl knickers on, get all the right treatment programs in place and clinical professionals aligned, and make it happen. I flew over there and sat in the classes, talked to the clients, talked to the staff, and then slowly, I started taking those that were lost to places where I knew, as a result of experiencing it myself, so that they would find the best of help required to lift them up.

The one and only positive thing my Nova experience taught me was to make bloody sure you've cased the joint out first yourself before sending anyone else there, so you can trust it's a place with the right people with the right program and the right intentions to help unwell souls. Because if nothing else is true, some people only get one shot at this treatment rehab process, and if a facility isn't offering you the best possible care, combined with excellent psychological understanding and tools to set you on your way, you will leave there and run for the hills with your substance of choice glued to you. You will never grace the doors of another treatment center for a very long time, if ever.

In 2017, through different sources, I met a clinician who worked at rehab in Thailand. I'd researched Thailand before. I'd looked at the benefit of treatment costs including travel, and it all pointed to an overall lower financial commitment to my client. Although that wasn't always the case, my concept was to get the best treatment, in the best environment at the best financial outlay for my clients, in that order.

## Simon

I had an old client from Capri, who was in his 60s constantly relapsing and suffering from serious health conditions due to his great love affair with Brandy. He experienced long-term depression and his sadly diminishing lack of self-worth, along with having a heart attack the year before which required stents placed around his heart. He was as good as gone unless I could get him somewhere long-term to at least sober him up long enough to let the tools and knowledge of what he had acquired catch up with him again. He reached out to me and asked for help. In his own words, he stated his fight wasn't over yet. I arranged for him to be placed in private detox for 12 days before departure, then the nurse and I flew with him to Thailand.

I stayed by Simon in treatment in this rehab in Thailand for around 7 days, meeting all the staff, getting to know the clinical team, the nurses, and talking with the other clients. I participated in the program, reassuring myself that this place had what it took to help my clients on their road to recovery. Simon regained his health and his reason for living a life without Brandy.

He has remained a very dear friend to me with his English gentlemanly ways and kind and generous heart, even donating leftover weeks that he had in this rehab to other clients of mine that couldn't afford to stay longer in treatment, but definitely needed to regain more solid footing before discharging into my aftercare. Simon remained sober for three years until a very short-lived relapse occurred in March 2020 of this year. He suggested that I include this story, for which I'm grateful to him. Relapse can happen even a few years down the track. In Simon's case, he had let all the tools of recovery slip as his mental health around depression increased. He was facing retirement and wasn't coping, so instead of reaching out and connecting to the right people and using what he knew from his own personal inventory, he reached out for brandy. He fell, and he fell hard. What he did have was the ability to immediately reach out again for help to those who care about him. He called our dear mutual friend Kimberley (Kimbo) and received instant and immediate care from her to stop, before it stopped him dead in his tracks.

I was in Thailand at the time, otherwise, I swear to God and he knows it, I would have turned up on his doorstep and verbally slapped him into next year. Kimbo's approach was a little gentler, but still, none of us mince our words when we have experienced the impact of what even a short relapse can do to those who suffer from Substance Use Disorder. When people reach rock bottom, all hope and chances of change are gone other than that one choice that is within them: TO STOP. Simon has backed up the pony and is in a really good state of mind again, receiving care and compassion the psychological way, rather than the alcoholic way.

I treat every single one of my clients with care and respect, with compassion and understanding, and over and above all else, uniquely. Every single person is unique to their circumstances surrounding how they found themselves at my door. In the same way, we all have different things that happen to us that create different mental health issues that create pathways to where a person needs to self-medicate with a substance to control the noise in their heads. Mental health is the most prominent in taking center stage. Not always, but 95% of the time. Very rarely do I come across a person who, when assessed by a psychologist doesn't discover that. For most of their lives, there have been these lingering issues that have been forging the way that they deal with their problems. It has impacted their relationship with themselves and their relationships with others. It has been holding them back.

I'm not a therapist, nor do I have certificates or degrees or lots of letters after my name. I'm just me. I'm a person who suffered from alcoholism, and other mental health issues and discovered through decent treatment, how to live a better life. Because I know alcoholism is there and I am able to manage it, I know how to take care of it psychologically, so I never get that need to numb again.

Some people never get the chance to stop the world and get off, to truly have the professional help to look inside themselves and revisit or investigate what is possibly wrong. I'm one of the lucky ones. I'm the best possible version of me now—someone I'm happy to live with. I'll never stop growing and learning and trying new and different things, but the bones of me are what they are now, and I'm at peace with that.

I've been called many things with the life I lead and the work I do. Navigator, gatekeeper, guide, friend, and Auntie, of all those I've walked beside through their journey of discovery. I don't call it a job as much as a lifestyle. I make enough to get by. I'll never be rich. I spend many hours weekly on the phone with people who are unable to seek private treatment and invest in researching their area to find what's around them in the public sector, giving them the knowledge to reach out and get the help of any kind. Mostly I talk to people from a place of deep understanding. I don't enter into or try and break down their personal underlying issues or enter into discussions on their mental health status. That's for the professionals. I know not to open the cans of worms, but I do know how to bypass that little fucker called addiction. I know how to reach in and whisper in people's ears, to talk to the well parts of their mind. Although overshadowed by an unwell mind, it's still there.  It's just in the background, waiting, waiting for the substance to take a long, on your bloody bike, holiday.

> *I know you, addiction, and I know*
> *many ways how I can break you.*

C H A P T E R  30

# *Intervention (or Interruption)*

## Real names used with permission

Interventions have played a big role not only at Capri when I worked there but, in my life, running Solace. I learned from the best, listening and learning about how Michelle did it, and taking my experience from all the many times those who loved me had tried to perform them on me. Whatever way they tried, none of it worked, because I wasn't ready to resign. So, I try to do interventions either differently or completely opposite of how they were performed on me. Along with Michelle's guidance, to begin with, I again started to use my own individual way of doing things. Sometimes all heads in our office would snap up from behind their screens in that office room full of therapists and me.

In the early days, I was often told, "you can't say that." But they soon learned the madness of my ways, especially when the person on the phone who was seeking the guidance of how they could help their loved one would call back, hand the phone over to the one they were trying to help and confirm that they truly wanted to enter treatment themselves.

It didn't always work. Some people would call and tell me that their parents or partner were going to leave if they didn't get treatment. They would say things like, "I HAVE to come to you." When I heard that, their name didn't go on the board immediately.

171

I needed them to want it for THEM, first. Otherwise, it was just a huge waste of money, and that person's chance of having an open mind to listen, learn, and accept was minimal. You can't help others if they don't want to help themselves. Nine times out of ten, a few months later, that person would phone again, and say, "I'm ready now."

It was a bit different when I started doing interventions face to face rather than directing the family on how to stage one. Just a little.

If you have ever watched the show Intervention on TV, you can get a hint of what I do. The way I interrupt people's careers in addiction is remarkably like that. Thankfully, to date, there haven't been many belly ups, but a couple of times I've been chased out the door with someone screaming at me. With one woman, the timing was way off as she had been mixing coke and alcohol throughout the night, so an early morning interruption meeting with myself and her broken adult children fell flat. She let me know that I was a pompous C***. I took real offense to the pompous part. We kept trying other ways after that. The last time I heard, her children had gone into the shadows, her marriage was over, and she had fallen deeper into the clutches of hell.

Two incidents really stand out among many. The first was a beautiful, but broken young woman named Emily, who fell on the sword of meth addiction (Ice) in Australia. She was released from a hospital with the doctor's understanding that she was coming home to where I was waiting with her supportive family. Horses were her passion. She loved competing in show jumping events in her old life before meth snatched it all away. I'll never forget the look on her face, or when she looked at her father and sister and cried thank you. She said, "Thank you for loving me enough to help me, thank you for not giving up."

We left on a flight to Auckland that afternoon into the care of a detox nurse. Then we all flew to Thailand a week later after she had stabilized medically and psychologically. Not all people stay directly in touch with me as they sometimes need to put time and space between their wounds and finding their wings. So, I stood back after a while and left her to learn to live in the world she wanted for herself. I'd watch her on Facebook. Oh, how my heart soared when I first saw the post of her on her horse at an event. Not long ago, she sent me a message of gratitude for being at her father's house that day and for navigating her into a caring treatment clinic that gave her the tools that allowed her find a way home to herself. The message was from her and her family letting me know that she had a life now, and she was happy.

Another one was the story of three sisters gathered for the love of their only brother. Along with his wife whom the sisters adored and who was directing this interruption, he arrived at the home of one of his sisters who lived nearby, only to be greeted by his entire family and me. When the look of registration and resignation appears on the face of someone who walks into a room, that is when I first believe I may be in the presence of a warrior. You see, if everyone is telling you that you have a tail, you should turn around and have an awfully hard look to see if you do. Rob knew. It was written all over his lovely, kind face. The game was up, and crunch time was here.

He loved a cold beer and a drop of fine wine. However, life long ago had become a party for one, and everyone in the family had become fragmented around his behavior. Their relationships had all but crumbled around him, little by little, including the one he had with himself. I can still feel the power of the love that was in the room that day. One by one, the sisters, and his wife, held him and asked him in their own words to give himself a chance, find some hope, and accept the help. They made it clear that if he refused, they would accept his decision but could no longer live with him or stand beside him. Thank God they didn't have to go as far as to say what their full conditions were. He shed tears and said, "Yes, I want it, I'll do it. I'll go."

Before people say yes, I always give them the outline of where we would go, what it would look like, and how I will be there with them every step of the way. Even after they have said yes, I'd normally wait 24 hours, to make sure in my mind that they were clear in theirs, that this is for them and they must go for themselves—no other. If they truly, deeply want the chance to change, they must seize it for themselves.

I walked outside of that interruption after we had finished, I got in my car, and for once in a long while, I cried as well. The shared force of love and connection to help someone you love so dearly was there in that house, and because of that, love won over addiction. He is well and content, calm and at peace today with his beautiful wife and children and his cluster of sisters who weren't about to let him go.

Today, when I talk with Rob, he never fails to ask how I'm doing first. It's not deflection; it's the type of person he is—always so kind and genuine. He simply lost his way along life's sometimes rugged path and turned to a substance to make him feel accepted and complete. That substance on that day in that house lost the battle against his will and the love of those that stood by and loved him. He finally came to accept that the substance and the path he had chosen to take beside it, had done completely the opposite.

I contacted these two people after I wrote of their stories. After all, it is their story. Although I played a part in it, the day that they arrived in their family's home and found me, a stranger sitting there, it was their love for their family and their strength and persistence that got them where they are today. They simply trusted me, then graced me with the honor of allowing me penetrate their darkness and letting me explain to them that I knew. I knew where they were. I knew where they were heading. All I asked of them, was to let me lead the way for a time.

> *I know you, for I've been you, and from*
> *this moment on, if you agree to walk with*
> *me, I'll be the one who leads you to a place,*
> *to make damn sure you never go back.*

After I had contacted them both, I stopped my walk down memory lane. I ceased writing for a while, went out to the beach, and watched the sun start to sink. I let myself get still and know.

*Be still and know that if you want to
chance change and beat this bastard, you
can and you will, by whatever means that
gets you there.  You can, and you will.*

And they did.

# CHAPTER 31

# *Sam*

## (real name and events printed with permission)

Sam called me when I was at a petrol station filling up my rental car on the Gold Coast of Australia. As fate plays its funny hand, I'd only jumped back in the car to grab my wallet, otherwise, I wouldn't have heard the phone ringing, and as he said later, if I hadn't answered, it may have taken him a very long time to call again.

He was soft-spoken and sounded a lot older than his age. He talked with absolute clarity around what he'd done, stating that he had made wrong choices, a lot, and that he was coming to realize deep inside him that he really wasn't meant to be doing what he was doing. He said that "meth had become a lifestyle many years ago, and it had taken over everything" that he knew he wasn't meant to be this person—doing hard drugs and living his life the way it had now become. He came across as a very introverted young man living a very extroverted life. When I finally got to meet him, his criminal charges, and the young man in front of me just didn't match up.

Sam was addicted to drugs of all descriptions, but mainly Methamphetamine, Meth/Ice, and Gamma Hydroxybutyrate (GHB) or G, but better known as the date rape drug. GHB is widely used these days in long-term Meth users as it can bring you down fast, and makes you sleep after days of being constantly awake and wired. GHB is highly addictive, much like alcohol, and it has to be extremely well managed medically to withdraw you off it.

Sam had been using some form of substance since mid-teens. So now at the age of 24, he was done in more ways than one. He went on to explain that he had a rather long list of charges against him, and as such, was having a long rest within the perimeter of his parents' home. The charges didn't make for good reading, and although he had been off his dial on drugs for every single one of them, they were going to be a challenge if we could get a court bail hearing, allowing him to leave the country of New Zealand and travel to the Rehab in Thailand where he and his parents had chosen for him to go.

I left Australia a few weeks later and returned to New Zealand, setting about working with Sam, his family, and his lawyer on a list of requirements and reports, stating, amongst other things, that I would be transferring him personally into Thailand and Rehab in Chiang Mai, where he would adhere to whatever conditions were laid out by the court.

I'd done this plenty of times before. I'd worked with prosecutors and probation officers, police, and lawyers, all with their best interests directed at getting a person who was suffering addiction, but who was also committing criminal offenses while under the influence, to find the best possible avenue for the best form of help. In short, we tried to get them off the streets, off the substances and out of courts and prisons, and into Addiction/Mental health treatment for help. I wish I could name these people of authority whose leniency has allowed a person to turn their lives away from one of entrapment, both mentally, and physically but also away from time behind bars.

Sam's court date for a bail hearing was set. His lawyer and I readied for a good shot at getting him out of court and pretty much onto a plane, with just a little paperwork and other official matters first. We both felt confident that Sam stood a good chance. Sam on the other hand was an addict, and although he seriously wanted to head in the direction of a rehab, his addiction took him in the direction of a pipe.

The night before court, as I was preparing the last of his admission details, he had been thrown in a police cell for breaking his bail by leaving the perimeter. Didn't help that he didn't go easily, and other charges were slapped on top of an already staggering lot.

Instead of appearing in court for a change of bail conditions, he was appearing for breaking them. I was gutted, along with his parents, as was Sam himself when he finally started coming down a few days later and was released back into his parent's care.

I came and went a few times over the next couple of months to Thailand, but always went to see Sam as soon as I was back. I drove from my home, which was at the southernmost point of Auckland, to his family home at the northernmost point. We would just sit and talk, and I'd sit and think about how and where and when I could get him help.

One particular night, I made a special trip up as Sam was showing increasing signs of going down, losing faith that he could change, and accepting that he may just carry on being the person he had accidentally become. He was on the tip of breaking bail again, which left no doubt in my mind that if he did and got caught, he'd no longer be parked up in the comfort of his family home, awaiting his court date - he'd be parked in jail.

Everyone had had enough, but my biggest concern was that I was going to lose him to the system and that he may not get a chance again for a very long time. He needed a chance to seek change. All charges pointed towards prison time, and I just didn't want to risk another week of that becoming a real possibility.

So, I asked Sam if I could get him into a private rehab treatment in Auckland, and if he would go. My skills in motivational interviewing were pretty polished by now, having come a long way from that day in Joy's office at Nova. I led Sam to believe it was his idea, that this place that did a three-week treatment was a really good option while we worked on continuing to get another bail hearing to get him into long-term treatment in Thailand. He decided that night that this was the best option for him, and I made fast tracks home to make it happen.

Guyon, Sam's lawyer is amazing. He had another bail hearing set within a few days, this time for a change of address within New Zealand; really go figure, a lot easier than a release from bail to travel overseas. The court day arrived, short of me parking myself outside

Sam's house the night before, I used everything in my verbal toolbox to make sure he stayed within his home perimeter that night.

The judge that day will probably never have any idea the difference he made in Sam's life, and in the lives of his parents, his brother, and all others who loved him. The judge said yes. He agreed on the change of bail address, and he agreed to the report that I had presented. That was the beginning of Sam's discovery—the discovery of who he really was and how he was really meant to live. That day was the end of the wrong path, and the beginning of the new, and the beginning of the rest of Sam's life.

Sam and I left court together, under the order of his new bail conditions, where I drove him directly to Capri Sanctuary and directly into the care of the man who had been the one to show me a way forward back in 2014 at Capri.

Brent had opened Capri Sanctuary in the country south of Auckland, 6 months after Capri Hospital had closed. Two of the nursing staff, Wayne, and Ruth, whom I worked with and adored from Capri Hospital had also gone on to work there, so altogether making a really good team offering a treatment of 3 weeks. It felt incredibly surreal handing over this young man that I'd really come to care for, to a team of people that I had not only worked with before; Brent and Ruth had been a big part of my own rehab days. I drove away that night, thinking, he's in the right place to start this journey of discovery, I believe he can do this, and at the same time thinking, thank fuck that 10 week battle of getting him good care and help, was over. Except it wasn't, not quite yet.

I went to see Sam ten days later after this initial medical detox period was coming to an end. As per my other clients, here standing in front of me was a person that I almost didn't recognize - his eyes sparkled, he'd put on weight and was no longer 6ft3in of skin and bones. Most of all, he had life starting to stir in him, hope and promise that maybe he could really do this was verbally present in his words, in his thoughts and in his determination to carry this treatment onto further green pastures, but in this case, amongst the rice paddies of Thailand.

Guyon and I continued to work towards another bail hearing where we could once again try for a temporary release from his bail conditions and get Sam on a plane over the ocean to continue a longer five-week term of treatment within a good psychology-based program. I had returned to Thailand as I now had another client Lizzie, who was due to discharge from Rehab treatment in the south of Thailand, and was joining me for a month in Chiang Mai while she found her feet again with me by her side.

As Sam's time at Capri Sanctuary came to an end, I worked with others to secure safe passage to Bangkok and then Chiang Mai, if by a very slim chance our request was granted.

The court hearing was set for 10 am in New Zealand, meaning 5 am in Thailand. I was up at 3 am pacing. I got a phone call from both Sam's mother and a text from Nina who was standing in for me in court, and who was packed and ready to escort Sam over; thank you Judge Gods, it was a YES. We'd done it - Sam had done it. That judge that day had faith that Sam could make it and allowed it to happen.

Sam flew into Thailand on the 20th of August 2019, directly from Capri Sanctuary where three weeks before he had laid down the pipe and picked up hope. Since then Sam has only continued to grow into the person he knew was inside of him. After his five weeks in rehab in Thailand, his mother Kate flew over to meet him, spending a week getting to speak with Sam's therapist in family sessions, getting to see where he had been, getting to acquaint herself with the son that she had raised and stood by, and finally getting to feel what hope felt like herself.

The courts continued to acknowledge Sam's commitment to change as he stood and acknowledged ownership for acts that he'd committed. The judge was able to grant some leniency towards Sam's sentences. He most certainly didn't get off scott-free, but he was able to continue with the freedom of working in the full-time job that he had now secured for himself. He was recently promoted to a supervisory role overseeing a team of others.

Sam is 26 years wise now. We talk over the oceans every Tuesday without fail, not because we have to, but because we want to. Any bumps he encounters, he will run through them with me. At well over a year free now, of the chains that bound him, he's got what it takes to continue on his own. In Sam's own words:

*"I now live in my life every day, as*
*opposed to just existing in it.*

I'm so full of gladness that I left my wallet in the car at that Aussie petrol station that day in May.

*Sam, I stood witness to the unfolding of the*
*special man that you have chosen to be today.*
*Your uniqueness and quiet knowledge that you*
*process beyond your years makes me so proud*
*to have been a part of allowing that to grow.*

Below is a letter that Sam's mother Kate penned a few months after Sam returned home from treatment in Chiang Mai. It's a beautiful and unique insight into how she saw Sam's Illness.

### *"love can conquer all."*

*Coming into this world alone your soul chooses its*
*family and in the form of a person you are born*
*into, you embark on a journey in this designated*
*lifetime. As a mother of a newborn, your instinct*
*is to take care of, to love, protect and nurture this*
*infant, guiding them through their early childhood,*
*instilling morals, values, and skills in the hope*
*that they will make good choices in their lives.*
*In our story when we discovered our son had a*
*problem with Substance Abuse, it was clear to*
*us he had made his choice of that pathway into*
*a dark underworld of drugs, violence, crime,*
*and living a life not resonating with the one we*
*had raised him to live. It was however a journey*

*he needed to embark on to learn his lessons only
to come out the other side a better person.*

*The decision we needed to make was do we as his
parents support him through these years of hell
or let him go it alone? Unconditional love as his
parents made that decision for us and we would
support him through this time however long it took.*

*A drug counselor told us after a session with
him, at a point we sought help, not our son,
he was perfectly happy living in his dark
world, that the only advice he could give
us was to have patience and when he was
ready he would seek the help he needed.*

*From then on, we got on board and went
on his journey to hell with him.*

*Most would say we were enabling him to
live this lifestyle and we were to a point, as
frustrating as it was to stand by and watch
him destroy his life and ours, but the choice
to do otherwise was taken away from us.*

*We loved him and could not walk away
from him when he needed us the most.*

*Substance Abuse Disorder is a disease and we
looked upon our son as being seriously unwell, and
mentally incapable of making good decisions. The
impact it had on our family over this time took its
toll, with us trying to maintain a normal life, and
keep the family intact. However over time the glue
came unstuck and the consequences of the life he
was living started to impact hugely on all our lives.*

*No one can prepare you for the personality changes
he had from daily using, the violent outbursts,
the physical fights he would have with his father,
and his brother all while under the influence of a
substance. The fear of living with this day after day
leaves you feeling like you are losing grip on reality
and being unwillingly sucked into his world.*

*These feelings of utter despair, overwhelming
sadness, and helplessness make you close
off from friends and extended family who
cannot fully empathize with you as they are
not walking in your shoes, therefore your
own journey becomes as lonely as his.*

*I reminded his father and brother several times
when they had got to the point where they had
had enough of living in his nightmare of a
world, that we were dealing with someone who
was mentally unwell and whose mind had been
taken over by the evilness of methamphetamine.*

*So we continued to stand by him through this.
We were judged by some, and possibly pitied by
some, our other son asked us again and again
as his parents "why could we not do anything
to fix the situation?" All I could say was that
we needed to be patient and when he was
ready, he would return to us one day healed.*

*Out of a journey like this comes a
light at the end of the tunnel.*

*It was during a time when he was living away
from the family for a few months in an undesirable*

*and unsafe accommodation that he finally gave
up and asked us for help to rehabilitate.*

*The absolute relief we felt was immense, it meant
our journey on this path was coming to an end
for all of us after what seemed like an eternity.
With our continued support, he researched and
discovered his own pathway to recovery and
allowed us to join him on this journey too.*

*This one was about rediscovering life again,
not just for him but for us as a family.*

*Investing in help from Denise (Seeking Solace) was
the answer to our prayers. Denise navigated him to
rehabilitation in NZ and Thailand and continues
to support his recovery through aftercare back here.*

*Only now we are finally able to move forward
with all our learned lessons on board, and slowly
put the pieces of our family back together.*

# CHAPTER 32

# *Lizzie*

## (real name and events printed with permission)

I was home from moving around the globe for a bit, so thought I would fly home to Queenstown, to my mountains, my lakes, and my friends for a while. As I was literally boarding the plane in Auckland, I received a phone call from a father telling me that he needed to talk to me about his daughter, to confirm to him that a rehab she had found online offered quality professional care and was the right place for his daughter to go.

It wasn't unusual that people would find their own way under their own steam to either the rehabs that I trusted, those that had proven to me personally that they ran excellent professional based programs. I was asked often by the CEOs of these rehabs to give my professional recommendation to those who wished to travel solo.

As I had two minutes to turn my phone off, I promised as soon as I landed that I would call back and answer any questions on what he and his daughter needed to know. I landed in Queenstown and immediately phoned Lizzie's father back. What he went on to tell me didn't shock me, though it rocked me slightly. Lizzie, unbeknownst to her family, had been suffering from severe depression and anxiety for several years, coupled with medicating on alcohol to help soothe what she didn't understand, and mask what she was doing.

I listened to his account of events that had happened the week before, and I reassured him that he was sending her to the right place. I explained what I did and how I did it, and the very next morning, I booked a flight back home.

Something in my bones told me that I needed to be in front of him, and possibly in front of her, if they were to collectively and safely get Lizzie to where she clearly needed to be, in the care and comfort of compassionate people who understood what she had just been through and to make damn sure it didn't happen again.

Lizzie woke up from a coma in the ICU of a North Shore Auckland hospital on the 5th of June 2019. She did not and still does not have any recollection of the events that got her there. Lizzie was found hanging in her home on the night of the 1st of June 2019 by her ex-husband. She was unresponsive when he cut her down. He resuscitated her, then she needed to be brought to life again by the paramedics, and then for the third time once they got her to hospital. Lizzie spent days in a coma, with her family aware that, for the time that she had been in cardiac arrest, her brain was starved of oxygen and may have left her with permanent brain damage. It didn't. She regained normal mental and physical function, and with that, the offering of another chance at living.

In the hours before, Lizzie was just doing her normal behavior of consuming large amounts of alcohol that long ago had become her hidden secret and mainstay. She had managed to keep her depression deeply hidden and her anxiety controlled by drinking alcohol. She was to everyone else a young 37-year-old mother, an early childcare teacher, and an incredibly bubbly and creative woman with loads of friends. Lizzie was always doing things for others. The problem was that she didn't do anything for herself.

She later learnt that she had sent a message to her ex-husband (their relationship had been long over). He was surprised by it and concerned enough to drive a decent distance to her house to check on her. Lizzie discovered after a few months of working with her Clinical Psychologist, Dr. Jones that with all the facts presented, psychologically she was in a complete alcoholic psychosis state when she did what she did. The trauma sustained would be blocked by her memory to help protect her in going forward.

The reason I have included Lizzie in my story is two-fold. First, she is a woman, a teacher, a mother, and a daughter who suffered depression and anxiety that she found by drinking alcohol. She thought she could cope with it. Nothing outstanding or remarkable happened until she psychologically cracked. Lizzie didn't want to show weakness by reaching out. She didn't understand that piling so many things up deep inside her head, then drinking to numb it, could lead her to do what she did. Secondly, she wants to share her story loud and clear—to let others hear. She sincerely hopes that it will help others like her, reach out for help sooner rather than later, before it could ever get to this, before it is too late.

Lizzie and I connected when we met a day after I flew back from Queenstown early. I met her father first, then she arrived for coffee after just having had her hair done. Again, like Sam, Lizzie's presentation and the recent events didn't match up. We didn't have too much to say to each other that first time we met. I just answered her questions about what it looked like to travel to Bangkok and then explained the pretty straightforward transfer down to the island. I know now that Lizzie was sitting there quietly figuring me out. She had a presence of not saying too much, but later, as I got to know her better, I could tell by her silence that her mind was running a marathon.

I wished them all the best for the trip, and told them to keep in touch with me if they ever needed anything. I hugged Lizzie, and said, "You've done the hard part now in acknowledging you need and want help. Everything will be ok from here."

I'd just got home when my phone rang. Her father asked if I could be ready to fly in 12 hours, that Lizzie wanted me to lead her there.

I stayed by Lizzie for quite a while once she had entered the sanctuary of treatment on that Thai Island. I kept thinking that it was too smooth, and something had to give. It didn't. As I got to know Lizzie better, I started to understand how such a catastrophic event in her life had signalled her turning point towards finally having a better understanding of who she had been pretending to be all these years.

The changes in Lizzie became clearer after her time in treatment. She flew up to spend some time with me in Chiang Mai. I started to witness her emotions present themselves as she felt them. If she was angry, she would express it. If she was upset, she had learned to let it out. When she was happy, well that was infectious and felt widely by those around her. She was finally feeling, and with that, the masks she wore for others and, most importantly, the mask she wore for herself, just fell away.

We remain in touch today, not every week or month, but I've got her number, and she's got mine. She's living her best life now, one day at a time. I learned a lot from Lizzie about how people who struggle with depression/comorbid issues can learn to lean forward and see their lives—their futures—with a far greater perspective. Lizzie overcame many things by firstly recognizing that she wasn't superhuman and in order to live a good life, she needed to matter the most. She had been and done and seen many things in her years to date, but one person she'd never really known was herself. I'm so glad that my bones told me to turn around quickly from Queenstown and return up north to see her. It was such a beautiful experience to watch Lizzie fluff her second set of wings, slowly raise her head up high, and learn how to finally fly.

From my early days of volunteering at Capri, and then onto working there, professionally receiving a really good educational understanding of Mental Health and Addiction, I have had the ultimate opportunity to meet some of the bravest, most inspirational, empathic people—wounded warriors, who had the strength to reach out, and say, "I can't do this anymore; I can't do this alone."

I can't, you can't, but together we can. That is how I see my role in what I do today. The human mind alone needs connection. Our emotions need connection, as do our bodies and souls. No one is meant to walk any of life's paths alone, especially when we find ourselves in troubled waters.

# CHAPTER 33

# *Families Matter*

Addiction likes company; it likes to spread its ugly darkness over everyone and everything. When it comes to standing by someone you love, care for, live with, or work with, it's a whole other layer of hell. Watching the person who matters to you slowly destroy themselves through abuse of a substance is like watching a horror movie on long play for years at a time. Excuses, lies, stealing, hurting, hoarding, repeat. It's unimaginable how someone who was clearly sane can turn into somebody almost overnight who clearly is not. What is the definition of insanity if not doing the same thing repeatedly and expecting different results?

As the addicted person becomes cleverer about how to achieve their same results, so do the others who try to help them achieve another healthier result. It's like banging your head over and over. While their behavior is numbing, you are also deeply hurting. As I've said, selfishness is one of the greatest traits of someone who is chemically addicted to a substance. The foremost thing their mind and body is telling them is to protect and secure, while yours is telling you to duck and roll.

As much as I've spent time with my clients, I've probably spent as much time with the ones who love them. Navigating a client into care and teaching them to understand how to learn to leave what's harming them behind is no easy task. Those who love them are left to wonder what the hell just happened and how they got here. Sometimes others need as much help as the person with the substance disorder. All the time, those that have stood by, need to be validated for what they turned into as a result of desperately trying to help stop the inevitable train wreck.

Instead of being a wife or husband, a mother, or a brother, they had to become a detective, a nanny, a friend, a foe, a gatekeeper, and often, an enabler. That word is not nice to hear, but it is a reality. This is how it works: You love someone enough so you start to adjust your emotional and physical life to run parallel with the life they are creating while addicted to the substance. They can't see that they need help, or they don't want it yet. The hallmark of addiction is to make you believe you don't have one, so they refuse to seek help.

When it gets to the stage of the train leaving the station, you are trying to lead a life on any reasonable, manageable level you can find. But your days, your nights, and sometimes your bank account is controlled by how the person is acting that day. You stay in a constant state of fight, flight, or freeze, very much like them, but on a different level. You're not addicted to anything harmful, but you become addicted to helping them while they are addicted to something that is destroying both them and you. So, you adjust or even give in. The mind cannot continue to fight what it's not able to change, so sometimes you begin to enable the person to simply have some semblance of calm and peace.

You turn off to them when they are out of it. You may tune in now and again when they are not. You may give in and let them have their wallet, even sometimes going and buying the substance for them. You become something you are not.

No one on earth deserves to be this bloody miserable, or live life this way, so eventually, the ultimatum time comes. You finally realize that you can no longer go on. You say to the addicted person, "You know I loved you once, or I still love you now, but I can't stand by and continue to cosign with your life of addiction. Worse, I can no longer stand by, and love you to death."

That can normally be crunch time for those with substance addiction and the person standing by. The bottom line is that it was never their fault, nor was it ever yours. It is the addiction that kills love. All you ever wanted to do is take them into your arms and fix it. But all the substance ever wants to do is take them out of your arms and kill whatever good thing they had going on in their lives.

I use the word "substance" that leads to addiction like it's a separate identity because it is. Addiction and substance use disorder refers to a disease that lurks deep inside us all. People have to try it often enough first for it to catch fire inside your mind second. That's undeniable. In the case of alcohol, it's a legal drug. So, everyone tends to use it.  In the case of drugs, some are so well designed that you only have to use them once to want more. Before you know it, the trap door is slamming shut. Anything that makes you feel so good once is addictive. Coke, for example, is the rich man's meth as it's referred to today. But it's no different from any of the others when you find its effects meet your needs and starts to make you believe it's the only way you can feel complete.

# CHAPTER 34

## *Mark and Kim*

Back in 1978, I was a full-time boarder at Enwood Hostel in Invercargill while I attended Southland Girl's High. I loved my boarding school days. Many don't, but it suited me. I liked the independence it offered, like a few of us girls leaping the fence and doing midnight runs to Snoopy's Fish and Chips, before upping it do marathons to the boys' hostel miles away. My first ever childhood boyfriend Brett was at school there. I have such beautiful memories of those sweet innocent times.

Kim was my cube mate for the full two years I was at school. We were total opposites in personality, but we really liked each other, enough to share a room with only enough space for two beds. This was where we spent those early growing years.

Kim and I kept in touch with each other after we went our separate ways from school. You can't live in a box like we did without it creating what was to become a lifelong bond. Kim left New Zealand at around 18, never to return to live. She first moved to America and, after meeting her future husband Mark, moved to his home country of Africa, eventually settling in Namibia, Africa. I stayed on in my home base Queenstown. I saw her again in 1990. Ten years had passed, and while I was marrying and mothering, she and Mark had set out to sail on their yacht for a look around the world.

What they didn't expect was Kim getting pregnant, and as she hit the six-month stage, she finally saw a doctor in the port of

St. Martins where she discovered she was hauling twins. Kim had to quickly return to New Zealand and Mark had to find a port to park their life and home. They eventually returned to the port and their boat and continued to sail until the time came to stay on land while the boys grew up. Mark and Kim returned to a new vessel, a catamaran in 2015. As they once again set sail from Africa to revisit their dream of a life exploring the world, just as they had done 25 years earlier, I was just a year into finding out what life was like sober.

Not all that glitters is gold, and this was representative of Kim and Mark's situation. They looked like they were having the time of their life that most would envy, but while the FB posts showed them sailing around countries with stunning waters, they were sticking close to a country where the religion and rulers forbid alcohol, so Mark had some time away from drinking. It was clear to me when things weren't so good with Mark anymore. He had always been the one who posted the stories of where they were heading and what they found when they got there. I swear Mark could write a post about a pole and make it sound like the most interesting thing you'd read in weeks. His storytelling is captivating, full of humor, full of facts, and full of his unique talent as a writer. Then the posts would stop suddenly for weeks. Others might have missed it, but I knew.

Kim started contacting me more regularly in 2016 asking for help and advice on how she could show Mark how his drinking was really beginning to affect her. As I became more educated in the underbelly of substance abuse and the mental health link, I shared with her what I was reading and what I had learnt. She did her research to try and get a better understanding for herself, so she could be better equipped with reasons to put to Mark about why he should stop.

This went on for a long time. Then Kim's messages started to become more fragmented. As Mark was falling deeper, so was Kim. She knew she was becoming co-dependent around Mark's unwellness, and she knew at times she needed to enable instead of being disabling. But no matter what she did, Mark kept on doing what the illness demanded of him - drink.

It came to a head in March 2019. They had been in Thailand waters for several months. Mark had even gone with Kim to have a look at the rehab I suggested that was on an island in the gulf of Thailand. His excuses about "why not" started to wear thin. They were so close, but still, Mark was holding back. I had just arrived back in Chiang Mai from New Zealand this day to a message from Kim resigning from the marriage. Mark had decided against rehab and she was just broken. Although she hadn't yet given him the news, her mind was made up. She was off the boat, over Mark, and out of the life that they had chosen together.

I was bloody fuming with frustration that after all this time, they were a stone's throw away from a chance to change. Instead, it was all heading south to Uglyville. Once I had rationalized what was probably going on in Mark's head, I sat down and sent a message to Kim, asking her to show it to Mark. I stated the deadly effects that alcoholism had on 'the others' like her. I ended it with, "It's not your fault, and it's not Mark's fault. It's the substance's fault. But it's entirely up to Mark now. What he does about it, is up to him now!, and it's no longer your burden to bear."

She showed him the message and confirmed to me that he had read it. A few days later, Kim got off the boat and flew to Chiang Mai where I was waiting to greet my dear friend. After 29 years, here we were, together again. And as we drove to a rehab where she was finally going to get her own good psychological care and direction, Mark was kayaking to the rehab that was nestled right above him. It had been there all along just waiting till he was ready and just waiting for him to decide it was over.

Eight weeks later, Mark and Kim set sail out of Thailand's waters, together again, reunited in their dream to live the life they had chosen. They both mattered, they both needed individual and separate care, and they both needed to go their own way to find understanding, knowledge, and acceptance to learn how to live their lives fully but together.

In the end, it's not so much what we drink or do drug-wise, or how much of it we swallow or smoke. It's all about how it affects you and others around you that really matters. If your behavior is shot and continually unbecoming of you while hurting others, you've got a problem.

I often think what it is like for those who are standing by a person who is suffering from this illness, especially in the early days before getting a client into treatment. It's like I'm watching one person deeply cut themselves, while I'm watching the other person who is standing by, profusely bleeding. It is madness, and it's the reality of where this can all lead.

I have had the profound pleasure of watching families reunite. There is nothing purer and more surreal than seeing a mother and daughter, a father and son, partners and friends look at each other with renewed promise and hope. I love to watch them interact and mend with each other, forgive and grow with each other after the storm is finally over and the clouds have started to clear. How lucky am I that I get to stand by and watch how their love for each other heals them.

*"To all I've had the pleasure of caring for, your names and places and reasons stay forever safe, locked up in a treasure chest in my heart. You know who you are. To those who have allowed me to walk and talk with you, you have honored me by trusting me to show you the way home."* – Denise

# CHAPTER 35

# *Happily Stranded in 2020*

In February of 2020, I flew out of Bangkok and over to Australia to meet up with my two boys, Joel, and Jack. Along with their lovely partners, we flew home to New Zealand and Queenstown together again. We had an extra on board with us who didn't take up a seat: my yet to be born grandbaby boy, Koa, who was hitching a ride with his beautiful Mum, Jacqui. We were returning to Queenstown after all these years as a family to celebrate Jackson turning 21 and to witness my dear friend Tanya's son, Luke, marry his long-time love, Elle. Four out of the five siblings finally got to get together again to celebrate their baby brother's big day, picking up like there had been no years or distance between them. Both occasions were, simply put, majestic.

This is what choosing to change gave me. This is what standing up and stepping up really meant: to be in the presence of those I loved so dearly and to be part of those moments with all those who loved me so dearly, rather than a sad memory and an empty chair.

I returned to Auckland a week or so later after spending some quality time with my Mum and Dad in Dunedin. I had time to pack up my house and sell off things that didn't really hold any value to me anymore. I started to go through a stage of not wanting to be burdened with so many material possessions. I was spending longer and longer times away with all my travelling, so I just decided to free myself of everything. I was due to leave in about ten days for Aussie again and spend more time with my growing family over there when, suddenly, the COVID siren started screaming, and I started running.

COVID's early signs of destruction started to appear in Chiang Mai in mid-December 2019. Shops and businesses were starting to really suffer, hotels were shutting down, and masks were made compulsory. Even on a flight back from Vietnam on the 24th of December, we weren't allowed to board without one.

Thailand heavily relies on tourist dollars. Its land of smiles and idyllic beauty makes it a popular destination for people from all over the world. But it's also not far from China. So, as it all unfolded in Wuhan, China, its effects were felt quickly in Thailand.

It was all over the news in South East Asia, and, although I was following it closely, I did not foresee what we now know has happened. When I flew into New Zealand on the 29th of February 2020, there was not a sign in sight relating to COVID, unlike 3 weeks later when I literally dropped everything, including ditching my car at the last minute to take the last flight back to Thailand before their borders closed. If I hadn't left New Zealand, I would have been trapped on the wrong side of the world and far away from two clients who were in treatment in Chiang Mai. I managed to get on the flight with all the correct paperwork that granted me passage, so I was on my way back to Bangkok until a stopover in Singapore signalled that I was not.

The flight that was to connect with another from Singapore to Bangkok was delayed, then delayed again for two days. I and hundreds of others struggling to get to their countries to seek shelter watched the boards constantly show "cancelled" status. I could write a book on the people I met and the situations they were in, but one man stood out, a very drunk Irishman. He wasn't annoying me directly, just telling anyone who would listen, his reasons for heading back to Thailand. Although he didn't have the proper paperwork, they were going to let him in. The state he was getting himself into, I was surprised they agreed to let the poor chap on the plane, let alone into a country. Everywhere I went in that large airport, he seemed to appear and repeat the same bloody story I'd heard an hour ago.

My flight to Bangkok finally showed up, 43 hours after I'd landed in Changi Transit Singapore, and 24 hours after Thailand's Government had closed their borders. The flight up was eerie, the huge plane almost empty, and I started to think maybe I should start coming up with a plan B. I always have contingency plans for everyone else, and mostly for me. But I just felt in my bones that immigration would see fit to let me pass with my six-month multi-entry visa, and my insurance card. I also had a letter from my doctor that I'd made a mad dash to see. I asked him to write the words "no evidence of COVID-19" all over the document, although I had to tell him how to spell it. This had been enough confirmation to allow me to board the flight in New Zealand and again in Singapore; I felt semi-positive it was going to be enough to see me into Thailand.

I can speak conversational Thai, but I can understand it more than I let on. So, after I got to the third line up in arrivals and heard what the newly appointed health officials were saying to each other behind their glass partitions, my confidence suddenly dived. It took about 30 seconds for me to be denied entry into Thailand with the repeated words and taps on the window pointing to a sign, "No COVID test, No entry." If you have ever been to Thailand, you'll learn one rule very quickly: you don't get loud, and you don't get aggressive. It's a sign of utter insult and disrespect to raise your voice, and it will get you absolutely nowhere. So, I tried to explain in Thai, "I'm not a tourist, I have a home up north in Chiang Mai" and on and on. It was enough for him to actually look at my passport full of Thai entries and visas, but not enough to get me to pass go.

It was about now that the sound of crying and panicked voices started to fill the air to the point that, when I took my blinkers off, I could see people everywhere on the wrong side of Bangkok setting up camp in arrivals. And for the first time in forever, I sat myself down, and I thought, ' Shit, what now?' My bags were on the other side, my clients were on the other side, and from my side, flights to anywhere in the world had been cancelled.

So, I sat, I waited, and I watched. For seven hours, I tried a different line but got the same result; I watched the staff change and I tried again with the same result. I did not have one clue what to do. And then, out of the blue, amongst the chaos that had become Bangkok arrivals area, I heard the drunk traveller first and spotted him next—my little Irishman, still a little worse for wear, but desperately trying to explain his saga to a Singapore Airlines representative. He had left the oil rig and started his transit back to Thailand the day before they had closed their borders. Technically this wasn't really true, but… minor details.

The borders were closed to anyone who didn't have a COVID test result of negative in their hands. Simple! However, I edged up to where he was standing with the poor woman who was trying to make sense of his accent and what he was trying to explain. I edged in a wee bit more, and then I jumped in and explained to her what he was saying, along with, "Oh yes, here are my details that show I too left New Zealand before the announcement was made." I hadn't, but again, I'd tell her anything to get myself on the other side of where I'd found myself now. She and I knew that the dates and times said otherwise. I grabbed the Irishman as she led us away from the chaotic scene around us to another health check area at the other end of the airport. Within 5 minutes, a person in a white coat looked at me and stamped my passport with a health clearance stamp which authorized me in. I saw the Irishman on the right side of Thailand, 10 minutes later. I wanted to thank him for getting pissed and saving my bacon, but as I was heading for the door, he was heading for the bar.

It took me a few days to overcome that one, but I had plenty of time to do this. Foreigners were now viewed as bringing the pandemic in, so laying low and self-quarantining was the safest tactic for me. I'd only been back a week when all shit hit the fan in the rehab where my two clients were happily tucked up. There are a lot of business and personal conflicting reasons around my not stating too much of what was going on with the management side of this rehab. But what I can say was that they weren't doing things in the right manner, and they were not correctly handling the massive COVID crisis. Most importantly, 26 clients who were now needing a safe passage home were not getting the proper support to do so. They were panicking with the Health Department's new rules and were clearly incapable of activating any decent contingency plan which I suspect they never had to begin with.

For the first and I hope the last time ever, I broke those two clients out of rehab. I phoned my driver and asked him to wait at the gate. I phoned them both and told them to pack their bags, get their passports, and hustle their butts out of there. I phoned their therapists who agreed I was on point. I phoned their families to explain the reasons for my actions, and then I sat back and thought once again, what next?

The jointly owned rehabs that I had used for the past 3.5 years both closed their doors a week later. All but one addiction and mental health treatment centre around Thailand had to do the same thing. The Australian and English owners as well as the management dealt with their duty of care of their clients with dishonesty and lack of responsibility. Their inability to pay one cent back to all those that had no choice but to leave before their treatment time was finished, sealed the deal that I would not ever be handing the care of my clients over to them ever again.

The story ends well for one of my clients. Nick and I huddled in a bubble and I introduced all the services into our home. We did hours of relapse prevention therapy along with the psychology of change with a wonderful therapist whom I'd worked with through the rehabs before. I introduced Dr. Gavin Jones, who provided months of one-on-one clinical therapy via Zoom. We had yoga, massage, and good food and fun. Really, in the end, Nick was the lucky one. He stayed with me for three months until things looked promising and his time to leave for home had come. However, the second wave was starting to hit sparking changes to quarantine protocol in New Zealand. Every flight we booked was cancelled to the point that even with the guidance of the New Zealand Embassy, there soon were zero available.

Finally, seven months after Nick had laid down the sword in February 2020, he left on one of the only flights heading back down under to New Zealand. He flew home to the bosom of his whanau (family) and towards the good life that he was discovering—a life that he knew in his heart and soul had been waiting for him. My last client for the foreseeable COVID era lifted his head, polished his wings, and flew to what and who he had always wanted to be, the life he deserved and was destined to have before addiction stole it away.

What lies inside of you, that which is destined to be, will never pass you by; it may just take a while to meet it. Like a magnet, it is being drawn to you day by day, pulled by an unstoppable force into your world.

My other client had been living in Thailand for around a year after her initial treatment. She was doing well until she wasn't. She struggled to cope without alcohol and although under excellent psychological care, she experienced several relapses. They say relapse is part of recovery. I don't agree. I say relapse is part of addiction. It's one of those statements that people will argue about, but here is my reasoning: sometimes there is quite a simple answer to an extremely complicated matter, just don't bloody pick up and start using it again.

If I'd learned that relapse was part of my recovery process, then my addicted mind would have found that to be the most excellent excuse to start using. I knew that I didn't have any second chances; my body was fighting so hard to live while my mind was telling me to give up and die. For me, the answer was simple:

> *Don't look back! You just don't belong there*
> *anymore, fight for your survival, surround yourself*
> *with people who know, use all the tools you have*
> *been given, embrace the grace to forgive yourself,*
> *have courage in your heart to get through the*
> *bumps, have faith, have hope, and you will win.*

She is part of the reason I haven't left yet;  I'm waiting and I'm praying to the powers that be, that she will find hope and try again— it's never too late. Like my friends did for me, I need to stand in the shadows knowing that I've done all I can. It's up to her now to want to try again, and when that happens, I'll be right here waiting to help her battle that bitch called addiction.

An old song called, "Those were the days, my friend" by Mary Hopkins keeps playing around and around in my head. It has been for a good part of the time; I've been looking back and writing about my life. The words speak to me about how this was my journey. Alcohol was my friend; my dearest friend was Sav. She took me to places in my own mind that I didn't know how to find without her. She calmed me, and she excited me. I could sing and dance forever and a day, as long as Sav was by my side. Until one day I discovered she didn't love me. She was a wolf in sheep's clothing. She smiled in my face while twisting a knife in my back.

I know that I matter the most now, and, before anything else I do, I have to work on me. I now know when to hold it in, when to let it out, and when to let it go.

I always make sure I take care of me first so I can continue to do what I love, be the person that others can love, and guide anyone who is standing up and reaching out, how to once again feel love.

Love and connection, peace, calm, and contentment—these are the elements that comprise of my life today. And when I forget to make me matter, there is always a glass door out there somewhere to remind me.


The end.

# *From a clinical psychologist's view*

## Written by Dr Gavin A. Jones.

I am a psychologist. I was employed at a private and luxury rehab in Thailand. I had been in that position for about five months when I first met Denise. At that time, I knew nothing about Denise, except that she would be visiting our rehab and attending one of my psychological groups. Denise sat attentively in my group. She offered a smile and would acknowledge specific points of interest throughout the group discussion. I interpreted this as a certain type of assuredness that only comes from personal experience, but I also sensed she had a gentle and sweet vulnerability about her. I have now known Denise for about three years, and I knew nothing of her life story until reading 'Poured me a Glass of Life'. I was surprised Denise was publishing her story because we had never really discussed our personal history in the many hours we spent together talking, in the past few years. Neither of us are particularly guarded people. It's just more that our conversations after the initial niceties of catching up are always more keenly focused on the clients Denise is asking me to support.

'Poured me a Glass of Life' beautifully and thoughtfully shares the human side of people's experience  battling alcohol addiction. It's a real-life timeline that graphically links the relationship between drink and personal struggles. Like so many in the field of drugs and alcohol, Denise's story is about coping with adversity. She candidly explores the meaning of disempowerment and the necessary changes needed to evolve one's concept of self. I knew when Denise provided me with the opportunity of a blank slate to conclude this book that I would need to use my clinical background to provide insight and psychological understanding on the topic of substance abuse. More specifically, I hoped to explore why the life of drugs or alcohol can be the choice people make, when it clearly brings such obvious suffering to so many. The reasons behind people's use of substances are complex and have a mixture of biological, psychological, and social underpinnings. In my chapter, I will take the opportunity to discuss the relationship between mental health and the misuse of drugs or alcohol. I think it's important to highlight what I observe clinically on a daily basis and how paramount psychological trauma is as a primary contributor to people's abuse of substances.

After writing her book, Denise explained that the process of telling one's story is cathartic because it helps to bring into focus the ambiguity of the past through a process of metacognitive thinking. Metacognition is a term often used in psychology to describe the act of thoughtfully contemplating and reflecting on the meaning of the past. This is an important process of sifting through thoughts, processes, feelings, and behaviours from times that were important in our emotional development. The metacognitive method can often be a very useful tool for helping individuals move forward in life by putting together pieces of the past. This is frequently accomplished through the writing of one's life story. It is human nature to tell stories to explain our internal and external world. It is an art that spans millennia. The ancient culture of storytelling can be found in paintings, music, and dance around the world. These unique and human-centered creative outlets allow us to define and enunciate the abstract inner workings of the mind in a concrete format that others are able to consider and critique. The art of creating and telling one's story is cathartic for the teller, as well as captivating and thought-provoking for the listener. In psychology, the story and its nature become the heart of the healing process.

In the profession of drug and alcohol services, people's histories, as well as their wanted life, often come within the frameworks of traditional archetypes or themes. Much like any novel or movie, people's personal narratives are almost always about 'overcoming the monster'. Defeating one's monster nearly always allows the individual to access the wanted life. This is the classic tale of 'rags to riches,' the story of being downtrodden and overcoming life's hardships. This is really a 'quest,' an invitation to the inner self to set off on a journey, knowing there will be adversities ahead. When a person's life has been hit with unexpected hardship, they must overcome that adversity before returning home to their core self. The tragedy is this story is so often one of loss and pain that concludes with heartbreak. The stories of people with drug and alcohol issues always contain adversities, which goes without saying. The challenge is we want to make the story have a happy ending. We want the confidence to know that people can slay the monster of drugs and alcohol and banish the disturbing memories of the past. Occasionally, in our professions, we hear about the patient who enthusiastically tells us that the monster is slain, only to discover that sometime later they were only, in fact, in the last chapter of a book about a tragedy.

Hearing about the loss of someone you have known due to difficulties with drugs or alcohol is upsetting. It is a strange feeling of helplessness, tinged with a wave of anger because it is not the whole truth. Indeed, drugs and alcohol are often implicit or explicit in the death, but understanding the loss of life for those suffering requires a closer examination of the complexity of the situation. The person's death can be accidental through an overdose. It can be intentional through an overdose, or it can come from a passive disregard for one's health that plays out over years and years, prolonging a slow but inevitable death. Other reasons for the loss of life may include the impact of intoxication on accidents. Risky behaviour often increases because of substance abuse and can include things like drunken violence, for example. We also need to consider the sickening disabilities that result from this risky lifestyle. The full truth is that I hold culpable not the individual, but the social spheres that create a psychological war inside their head. The person often turns to alcohol or drugs, searching for the simplest means of peace they can find.

Working life in Thailand as a British psychologist was a cultural change from my previous role, where I had been employed to work in a female prison. The women we cared for were typically working-class, mentally unhealthy, detained for therapeutic retribution, low educational attainment, and perhaps the least privileged people in society. The patients in the rehab here in Thailand in contrast, were willfully in treatment, international, affluent, educated, with mainly complaints of anxiety or depression. Most looked reasonably healthy with only a glimmer that they were unwell, which I think was due to the quality of their attire. Ironically despite all of their opportunity, they too were anything but privileged. I have never met a privileged person who has had a drug and alcohol problem. Perhaps it is because the drug and alcohol issue always comes with an underlining mental health difficulty, ascending from the unprejudiced randomness of life's adversities.

In Thailand, the patients would obsessively discuss their principal complaint around their psychological treatment. They wanted nothing more than to end their unhealthy relationship with drugs or alcohol. Even with their reasonably educated backgrounds, most were uninformed about the nature of their poor mental health and its relationship to their substance abuse problems. The correct psychological term used to describe someone with a mental illness with a co-occurring drug or alcohol problem is a dual diagnosis. Although mental illness for most people doesn't involve an obsession with drugs or alcohol, drug and alcohol issues are often driven by an underlying mental illness. In prisons, the rehab world, and medical speak, drug and alcohol misuse are commonly referred to as 'addiction'. One who has an addiction is an 'addict,'. The term addict has almost become a vernacular term in our field to refer to the dysfunctional compulsivity and cravings exhibited by the patient for substances. All too often, there are a few too many connotations within the term addiction or addict to signify the accompanying mental illness.

I never like using the word "addict" because nothing is complimentary or encouraging about the label. It implies one is forever at the mercy of an addiction, something not at all true. It also implies an almost biologically predetermined state for the unlucky some. With this false assumption comes the idea that some percent of the population is just lucky not to suffer from this affliction. I have always thought "traumatized" would be a more accurate description. The word "addict" permits the avoidance of the truth, the real truth that traumatic experiences are what explains the person's dual diagnosis. Trauma is a subjective experience because what is distressing for one person may not be distressing at all for another. In its original Greek meaning, trauma denotes an injury to the body, and with time it has developed to mean an injury of the mind. The term has become associated with war and conflicts. Yet, the majority of people who suffer trauma are not veterans. They are ordinary everyday people who have experienced adverse events in their lives. Around the globe,  these people number in the hundreds of millions.

In my work, I explain trauma as the occurrence of an adverse event that, in that moment, makes life take a divergent path. The event transforms life from the expected, the normalcy of day to day, to something unrecognizable. This adverse event causes a shock; the individual then attempts to make sense of this new reality. They try to reconcile the discrepancy between the expected narrative and the one that exists because of this trauma. Traumatic events are so often the earlier chapters to many people's stories of substance abuse who enter the still stigmatized worlds of mental health hospitals, rehabs, and prisons. These institutions are the holding services that manage what is overwhelmingly traumatized adults who were psychologically, emotionally, or physically victimized by predators as children. The truth is that these people are tormented by their pasts, which are still haunting them. People can only cope with so much suffering before they psychologically rupture. This rupture will lead them into the hospital, rehab, or prison. This psychological suffering will so often present itself in the form of an unusual mental health condition, compulsive drug or alcohol use, unusual behaviours, or criminality.

When I was working in Her Majesty's Prison Service, it was uncomfortable to learn about the depressing frequency of childhood emotional, psychological, and physical abuse that had occurred among so many of the inmates. Most disconcerting was learning about the frequency of childhood sexual violence of dual diagnosis cases residing in jail. In the English-speaking world, prisons contain high numbers of people regarded as dual diagnosis. The rates of inmates who have experienced childhood sexual victimization are as high as ninety percent in some institutions. In drug and alcohol rehabs, it is believed that around eighty percent of the women and seventy percent of the men have experienced childhood sexual violence. In broader society, there are estimates that one in five children are subjected to sexual violence, and the median age of victimization occurs at the age of twelve. These figures may be surprising for many to read. However, when people understand the impact of childhood sexual violence on mental health, it is then clear why people act unusually as adults.

The symptoms of psychological trauma in adults are often presented as the comorbidities of depression, anxiety, insomnia, nightmares, disassociation (feeling detached from oneself or the world), emotional instability, intrusive thoughts, self-destructiveness, self-injury, suicidal ideations, substance abuse issues, intrapersonal and interpersonal conflicts, as well as "negative affect," which is the experience of strong emotions such as fear, guilt, shame, and disgust. These are also the symptoms seen frequently in mental health hospitals, rehabs, and prison services the world over. The symptoms of trauma can also be seen more mildly in the form of unusual but everyday personalities. The specific and peculiar way in which people interact with their world. The coping is not always drugs or alcohol, yet there is often a compulsive want for a self-destructive soothing. Trauma can be seen visibly in the eating behaviours of the morbidly obese, the anorexic, or the bulimic as well. Trauma can drive the illogic of the obsessive gambler, the promiscuous motives of the adulterer, the complexity of the transgender, the reasoning for selling one's body, and the compulsive washing of hands until they are sore. Of course, many people will exhibit these unusual behaviours without traumatic pasts, but often in psychology, we learn that unusual behaviours usually require exceptional circumstances to develop.

The self-destructive soothing behaviours associated with trauma, are of discernible concern for the individual, their loved ones, as well as drug and alcohol therapists. Most therapists focus treatment on the ostensibly obvious components of substance abuse. This entails strategies that provide structures which may help minimize the behavioural harm associated with the abuse of drugs and alcohol. Therapists often can become unhelpfully obsessive in their desperation to minimize the behavioural risks associated with substances, and will sometimes employ treatments that become less and less clinically effective. Therapists can develop complex avoidance strategies that virtually render the individual's return to daily life useless. Leaving them fearful, withdrawn, and scared to even see an advert for alcohol on television. The strategy to simply repeatedly discuss the person's behavioural chaos while intoxicated as a means to shame or guilt them into abstinence is not impactful in the way it may be intended. To the reader, maybe these examples of interventions seem like common-sense, as surely you throw everything at such a challenge, even the kitchen sink when times are desperate. Clinically , however, most interventions will do little to prevent the psychological and physiological urges that are the precursors to their using substances. The cure does not lie in the individual's benevolence as they attempt to develop tools to slay the monster of alcohol and drugs. The means to slay the monster is in confronting the disturbing memories of the past head-on, without any complex tools. The only thing required for this intervention is just the patient's honesty and desire to change.

Improving mental health in dual diagnosis clients helps reduce the individual's need for intoxication as a means to remedy their emotional distress. Dual diagnosis treatment requires the management of psychological trauma, alongside providing workable solutions to improve the quality of the person's life. The more content the person is, the less distress they will experience. The less distressed the person is, the less they require a remedy for their distress, as it settles to a level that is more emotionally manageable. It is quite a simple methodology. After all, the patient knows fully well that they have an issue with drugs and alcohol and that they need to stop it. The way to help someone stop is to support them in exploring the meaning hidden within their substance abuse. This is not about the management of the surface level issues of alcohol or drugs, or medicating someone with antidepressants. This is about the strategic targeting and treatment of the original trauma's more profound and causative factors. Effective psychology provides a voice to the vulnerable, a voice to that small child that lays sleeping deep within. Allowing the person to talk about the unspoken for the first time, to explore their pain over and over again, until the symptoms of their pain dissipate, helps to unwind this trauma, and allow it to escape. This process gives them a safe space to recall the saddest and darkest of memories from their past without applying the emotional reactivity or the uncomfortable negative impact of the experience in the present.

The telling of the patient's personal story with corrective cognitive, emotional and behavioural feedback from the psychologist encourages the development of positive self-belief, courage, resilience, empowerment, self-compassion, respect, and determination. This combination allows the patient to find hope for change in the future. Many psychologists are fearful of exploring the patient's past when they know there have been upsetting life events. Psychologists can be worried that they will cause harm or re-traumatize the patient. It is evident from a psychologist's perspective why they would have this concern, as they enter the profession to do good and not to cause harm or distress. Successful trauma therapy allows the patient to safely experience their pain, through the telling of their story and cathartically sharing their emotional experience. I ask every patient who discusses their trauma if they would recommend this process to the next patient. To date, one hundred percent of people have suggested the treatment, and many have said it was lifesaving because sometimes the pain of the past is unbearable enough not to want the future. As Nietzsche said, "He who has a 'why' to live can bear almost any 'how'," meaning that when people have a purpose or a reason for living, it is only then that they can better tolerate life's adversities.

When telling their stories, many dual-diagnosis patients will attempt to understand the 'why's' and 'how's' of the process of making a better life. As they do this, they begin to question the chaos of their past choices. Psychologists are there to listen, guide with reason, and provide explanations for some events that may seem inexplicable to the patient themselves. This act of giving space helps to minimize their anxiety or ambivalence towards their past. One explanation that can help someone understand poor past decisions is best illustrated by the phrase attributed to Dick Swaab, the former professor of neurobiology at the University of Amsterdam, who simply said, "we are our brains." In other words, and perhaps too verbose for Swaab, this means that in stressful situations, a person's thinking and perception of the experience may change depending on the neurological variations of our unique brains and executive functioning. The executive functioning is essentially the part of the brain that includes the frontal lobes, which have neuronal network connections to areas like the cortical, subcortical, and brainstem regions involved in decision making. Disinhibited executive functioning supports good planning, rational decision making, reasonable impulse control, better memory, and it drives behavioural motivation.

Conversely, too much stress causes an inhibition to the executive functioning, meaning that planning, decision making, impulse control, memory, and motivation can be impeded. This may ultimately hinder the individual's ability to learn from their errors rationally. The relationship to stress and the impediment of the executive functioning is in part, thanks to human evolution and our cave-dwelling ancestors. They provided us with the neurobiology of stress and trauma. In its simplest form, stress is how humans respond to demanding stimuli via the hypothalamic-pituitary-adrenal axis, also known as a stress axis. An axis that helped our ancestors adapt to their ever-changing environment. The ones that adapted were the ones that successfully survived to pass their genes on to the next generation. When the brain perceives a threat, it was beneficial to make quicker decisions because more extended decision making may increase the time spent in a vulnerable situation.

These days the stress axis can become dysfunctional because we can experience stress from non-threatening life events such as forgetting someone's birthday. Perhaps this stress would be better served, for example to help us navigate crossing a busy road when the pedestrian lights are malfunctioning. People who have experienced traumatic episodes, such as childhood victimization, can often have severe and persistent stress because the brain believes it is at continual risk of repeated victimization. In other words, the brain believes that if trauma has occurred in the past, then it will most likely happen again in the imminent future. It is as though the busy road we are trying to cross has no end in sight, and we are nervously just existing in the middle, going slowly step by step, and just waiting for the impending collision. Therefore, for someone who is continuously revisited by the persistent stress of past trauma to the point where it impedes executive functioning, drugs and alcohol, and chaos often are a natural antidote. This constant stress, which leads to poorer cognitive and behavioural outcomes, may impact all areas of life. If you add intoxication from drugs and alcohol into this process, it quickly becomes clear what is behind the individual's seemingly unreasonable chaos.

The brain of the dual diagnosis person will attempt to provide reasons for what they are experiencing. This often comes in the form of beliefs, attitudes, or rules to help free them from the unwanted experience of stress. The remedies to the pressure are often implicitly driven by an evolutionary rewards system, which provides relief when a threat is avoided. In the past, this helped our ancestors to stay alive. It is a helpful evolutionary mechanism that ensured our ancestors evaded danger. When they encountered a tiger and managed to evade it, they would receive relief for evading the threat. Our ancestors' distant cousins who experienced curiosity when seeing a tiger, and chose to investigate further, would have had less opportunity to make babies and pass their tiger-curious genes forward as they would have more often than not been eaten. Today the same evolutionary system is at play, but the threat is not the tiger. The danger is that the attempt to avoid perceived discomfort, either from an internal physiological event or an external emotional experience of trauma. The result is often more dangerous than any tiger would have been. The avoidance of this perceived threat is manifested in the form of alcohol or drug use as the primary means to avoid stress. This pattern of avoidance will have the unfortunate consequence of positively reinforcing the using behaviour because the threat of discomfort can, in fact, be temporarily relieved.

The conscious narration that a dual diagnosis individual may provide to their subconscious in an attempt to make sense of their avoidance of the distress they are experiencing can present itself in the form of the development of behavioral rules. This might include such self-talk as "when I drink, I feel comfortable (to be safe); therefore, when I am uncomfortable (to be unsafe), I need to drink (to feel safe)." The stress is often further exacerbated by negative, more profound core beliefs about our own self-worth. In the dual diagnosis patient, core beliefs are mainly hatched from the adversities of childhood traumas. This means that the patient will discuss inherent core beliefs such as "I am vulnerable," "I am guilty," and "I am disgusting" regularly as part of their own personal narrative. Each belief is likely dependent on the nature and meaning of the instigating traumatic event and may become a self-fulfilling prophecy. For example, the belief "I am disgusting" may be attached to the attitude to behave accordingly. I think, therefore, I am, and as such, this dictates that "I am disgusting; therefore, I need to be disgusting." The core belief and the associated attitude can also explain the unpalpable behaviours that occur in dual diagnosis patients. This can begin to explain why someone may have a total lack of regard for their poor personal hygiene, their unusual or unsafe sexual practices, the choice to drink until humiliatingly soiling themselves, putting an unhygienic needle in their arm, or the unnecessary cruelty or vulgarity towards a loved one.

It is crucial to see unusual behaviours with a degree of mitigating empathy and rationale because the traumatized or stressed self is not the true self. It is not the person who they would have been if the unthinkable did not occur. No person wants to feel disgusting. The true self is not the suffering dual diagnosis patient. It is the person who understands that coherent steps towards an ordered and contented life are possible.

When I described the importance of sleep to human health in my psychology group, I referenced Hippocrates (Aphorism, LXXI), who believed that "disease exists, if either sleep or watchfulness be excessive." Denise knowingly smiled at me as I spoke. She has personal experience that gives her a sense of assuredness in critical factors that impact mental wellbeing. In her memoir, she describes in detail how this assuredness came to be as she faced the adversities in her life and ultimately found empowerment in her successes. As I have gotten to know Denise, I stand by my initial observation of her character. Now though, from reading her story, I can perhaps understand a little more about the psychology of her personality.

Denise is someone who presents as though she is balancing herself between the traits of an extrovert and an introvert, although she is not an ambivert in the true sense. Denise is learning more and more how to become the gregarious person that was obscured over the years due to traumatic life events. Denise is naturally comfortable around people, gaining energy through interpersonal interactions and conversations. Even more so when she is interested in the other person, she will become more emotionally positive and zealous. Denise's introversion traits were also most likely simply passiveness arising from dysfunctional agreeableness. By overly tolerating other people's poor behaviour for years, she began to lose her ability to assert her voice due to interpersonal anxieties and lack of self-confidence. Denise must have experienced many difficulties in managing her intrapersonal and interpersonal relationships. She would continuously contend with weighing up and grading her own personal rights over others' comfort. This challenge is all that much greater to negotiate because of her strong sense of compassion and empathy towards others.

I find Denise to be energetically conscientious, thoughtfully working on her personal goals, with a high degree of determination to achieve what she has planned. Denise takes particular pride in accomplishing her objectives, her responsibilities, and most importantly for Denise, maintaining her promises to herself and others, as she is inherently loyal. Denise makes a concerted effort to be humble, polite, and courteous, which you can see in her dutifulness to her relationships with other people, even strangers. I also believe that Denise is somewhat neurotic or anxious and understandably so from her life experiences. However, Denise is perhaps just more aware of the fragility of life and loved ones than other people. Denise's anxiety is also founded on deep empathy and compassion for other people, their wellness, and her want to ensure their successes. That trait of empathy is draining for Denise. It requires stress to always be thinking about others, which I would conjecture may result in the neglect of acts of kindness towards herself. Meaning, Denise's high state of empathy leads to higher levels of nervousness, sadness, and irritability. The belief that she can always do more for others is exacerbated by the conflict she experiences when her empathy is unreciprocated. However, she may not articulate this because Denise believes that 'silence can be golden' and most helpful at times.

Denise is also open to new experiences with a strong desire and curiosity to learn. Denise has a creative imagination, and she is an innovative and original thinker. I believe Denise is gifted with two types of thinking. One is 'divergent thinking,' meaning that when a problem arises, Denise can creatively provide many workable solutions to a problem. The second is 'convergent thinking,' where Denise will develop the optimum solution to an urgent issue under pressure. Denise also has a high degree of self-awareness that allows her to be easily approachable. There is no ego because Denise is willing to accept and take on board new ideas and information and learn and amend her beliefs based on the deep understanding of her own life.

I am curious to see what is in the next chapter of Denise's story of 'Poured me a Glass of Life.' I believe that Denise's calling is to be involved in mental health and drug and alcohol issues. So, I would like to see her continue supporting and helping people suffering from life's adversities - people who want to slay the monster inside their head. I believe she will continue to be wonderfully supportive of the affected loved ones who suffer in familial ways. Denise's success in drug and alcohol services is because she has such a loving ability to help someone feel supported and safe quickly. It is an innate part of her personality. Like her mother, a maternity nurse, Denise is also natural at caring for other people's children. I do sometimes wonder the extent that Denise is aware of her compassion and kindness, but perhaps she may realize from reading her own book that just like in the Capri Hospital, there are 'little Florence Nightingale's everywhere.'

# Denise Cloughley
## Author

A born and raised Kiwi, Denise first found success as a Casting Director, working in the Film Industry for 20 plus years. With a group of close friends, a loving family, and a wide social circle, she thrived in social situations, where her warm, bubbly personality and friendly spirit helped her make connections quickly. After a long and painful struggle with alcohol and several attempts to get sober, Denise finally found a treatment that stuck and chose life over alcohol. She quickly went on to establish a business helping others overcome similar issues with Mental Health and Addiction dependency.

Poured me a glass of Life was written accidentally when Denise found herself one morning needing to express an angry sadness at the brutal and often fatal disease of addiction. Starting to ponder some more as a typhoon passed over the Southern Islands of Thailand, where she was staying, she just as she states, did a Forest Gump, and didn't stop writing.  18 days later, she closed her computer down to realise, maybe she's just written a book.  Slowly heading back north to the city and mountains she loved in the province of Chiang Mai, with a completed manuscript of her journey and that of others, she simply felt it in her bones, that this is a story that has to be shared.

What if one person can read the message of strength and hope, not only around addiction and mental health, but around believing anything is possible? If you simply believe you can do it, you will do it. Denise spends her time living between New Zealand, Australia, and Thailand.

# Dr. Gavin Jones,
## BSc (Hons), MSc, DHealthPsychol
### (Contributing author)

Practitioner Psychologist, Facilitator

Gavin is a highly qualified British clinician and trained practitioner psychologist registered with the UK Health and Care Professions Council. He's been involved in the field of psychology and mental health for almost twenty years across a wide range of settings, with particular interest and significant experience in helping people who present with anxiety, depression, psychological trauma, suicide ideation, personality disorders, psychosis, medically unexplained symptoms, drug and alcohol misuse, and personal and relationship problems. Gavin believes that careful exploration of our personalities will allow us answer the question 'who am I?', and that learning about self and personality can become a liberating, meaningful, and therapeutic experience. His ability to encourage people to find resolutions to their deeper psychological and emotional issues has helped countless people to release the emotional distress that affects their everyday lives.

Gavin is Welsh and is presently based in Mexico where he spends his working life as a Practitioner Psychologist. Denise and Gavin have worked together for the past 3 years, helping all those deserving souls find direction, answers, contentment, and peace.

I met Robert in 2019. He had chosen to go to the same rehab in Thailand as Kat. Hence, Kat and Robert, along with 2 others, Karen, and Jess, all became firm friends.

Robert and I found friendship in humor, and similar views. Really, we are just kindred spirits over this, anxiety, shitty underlying issues, addiction, bastard of substance addiction thing. Robert hails from Scotland and the UK, and lives in Cambodia with his husband and soul mate Sop. I felt it was befitting to conclude "Poured me a glass of life" by sharing Robert's blog on what his first year of sobriety looked like.

# One Year
### By Robert Common
### August 2020

One year. It can seem like a drop in the bucket of life, or like an entire lifetime lived in 365 days. What if one year ago you began your sobriety? What changes have happened after being one year sober?

Recovery always involves growth, and a lot of growth can happen in a year. Without the blunting effects of addicting behaviours, every day has involved facing life with a much more realistic outlook.

At some point in the past year, you've experienced a sudden appreciation of something that's been unnoticed in your life for a long time. Perhaps it's how good it feels to have the sun's warmth on your face, or to hear the sound of your daughter's uninhibited giggle as she watches her favorite TV show. Maybe it's the refreshing tang of lemon sorbet without the interruption of nicotine, or tender pillow talk with your partner after an outing that didn't end in being drunk.

Whatever that first moment of awareness was, it held the hesitating promise of more moments to come. Because in that first year, there are many times when you weren't certain of your recovery. When you questioned the possibility that you could get to that one year of sobriety. And then you experienced the next good moment, and then the next.

After one year sober, your body has been through some major changes. At first, there were some horrible days (or even weeks) as your body slowly processed and released the toxic substances it was carrying. For many people, the physical withdrawal symptoms were agonizing, and the first few weeks left them feeling exhausted and disheartened. But as those toxins left your body, you began to feel healthier.

You might have been pleasantly surprised when you started sleeping better. And, of course, better sleep led to more energy and mental clarity. As your body stopped struggling to find balance during the constant exposure to toxic substances, you may have found yourself feeling recharged—without even taking a day off! It may have been your first year without coming down with every cold and flu virus that went around.

During the past year, you had to find new ways to spend your time that didn't involve activities associated with your addiction. Maybe you reconnected with things that used to bring you joy. Often recovering addicts rekindle their joy in running, swimming, playing instruments, and cooking.

Others find new activities and hobbies that fill previously unmet needs for physical activity, personal connections, artistic expression, and meaningful contributions.

Many people in recovery decide to make meditation a part of their daily routine after trying it for the first time in the early days of their journey. Enriching volunteering is another activity that becomes both part of the healing process and part of a healthier happier lifestyle.

The first year sober wasn't all 'rainbows and sparkles'. There were some very challenging days and weeks. Times when the journey felt impossible, times when surviving life without addictive substances seemed like too big of a challenge, and times when the consequences of years of addiction felt too heavy to bear.

We hope that these times remain in your memory—not as a negative thing, but as a reminder of each barrier that you've survived and overcome. Choosing sobriety will always include remembering where you've been while celebrating every new milestone that marks the path you are on now.

In the past year, you've seen a change in your relationships. Those based entirely on sharing addictive behaviours are no longer the centre of your personal circle. The superficiality of these became more obvious without that one shared interest. But even losing superficial relationships is still a loss.

You may have spent time in counselling or learning new ways to initiate and experience healthy relationships, and you've had to relearn how to be in a variety of situations sober. Maybe you've rekindled some of the best relationships from your past—ones that weren't compatible with addictions but are very compatible with sobriety.

Having relationships with people and *not* trying to hide an addiction has given you a new way of relating to others—with honesty and authenticity instead of deception and pretending to put on a brave face. During the past year, you may have had the opportunity to make amends with some of the people you hurt when addiction dictated your choices. Some of those people may be slowly beginning to trust you, perhaps for the first time.

Sometime during the past year, you began to get to know your real self. Without addictions masking who you really are, you started to learn truths about yourself. Maybe you found out you're an introvert who thrives in one-on-one connections with people. Or maybe you found out you love trying new activities where you'll interact with people very different from the ones you used to spend all your time with.

You've also begun to take responsibility for your own care and maintenance. You're learning to value yourself. This part of the journey can be pretty challenging. But at one year sober, you are starting to enjoy taking care of yourself and you're conscious of how good it feels to know you can meet your needs.

Speaking of responsibility, it's another thing that's been changing in the past year. While you have taken responsibility for yourself and your choices and behaviours, you've also worked on not taking responsibility for others. You're realising that it's not your fault when other people make mistakes, and this realisation is life changing.

Most addicts share a history of trauma, and they've spent years feeling responsible for other people's actions. But the more you've released that unhealthy attachment to other people's choices, the more empowered you feel over your own life. After a year of sobriety, you're getting better at saying no to people and situations that aren't right for you.

You're also learning to feel good about the choices you make. What a surprise! After years of regretting or defending your choices, you're now feeling proud of what you choose! The very act of choosing sobriety every single morning is a reminder of how life-changing (in a good way) your choices are. Speaking of mornings, you're also waking up every morning with a clear memory of where you are now and where you were last night. One year sober doesn't mean last night wasn't an embarrassment (although it often does); it means last night's choices were made completely by you without substance impairment. That's a big deal!

Celebrating one-year sober marks the sum of hundreds of little changes that you've made over the past year. And those little changes really add up. This might be the first time you take an inventory of where you've come in the past 365 days, and say, 'Wow, I didn't notice how much better things had gotten!'

And one of the best things about one year sober? The mystery and excitement of how many more good things are going to come in the next year!

# ACKNOWLEDGMENTS

I say that writing this book was the easy part, as it was never really meant to be a book. I didn't have any intention of even writing a grocery list 10 minutes before I started this on the 8th September 2020. So, to write an acknowledgement of those that have helped me to even be present here on earth to write anything is so huge, and slightly daunting.

It is my wish to thank and acknowledge those that have made a manuscript move forward from a, "that was an interesting 18 days" to an actual real book.

I would like to thank my first husband Greg Webb, my mainstay and port, for the moment when he called after I had sent him the final manuscript, and said holy shit, do you realise you have just written a book. It was about then that I accepted that I had done just that. Along with his lovely wife Alex, they have been nothing but a positive reinforcement to keep me moving towards print. Followed closely by my Mum, Pat, my sister Rob, and my best friend Nelly who collectively have had their ears burnt with all my phone calls from Thailand. Nelly and Tim, your unwavering guidance has been priceless, I know that this book would not have been possible without your constant support and understanding.

This group of people have never left my side through the now daunting process of what came next with self-publishing. To my beautiful daughter in-law to be, Jacqui, for your encouraging and uplifting words as you read through the manuscript.

To Kat's parents and brother, Karena, Ian and Michael, for graciously blessing and fully supporting me by granting me the right to keep Kat's real name and profession. For not asking me to leave out or change any part of the first chapter as I wrote it on that day that Kat left this earth. It was once I had eventually communicated with Karena, and after I had sent her the first chapter, did I feel it deep in my bones, that "Poured me a glass of life" was worthy of becoming a book. In Karena's words, "If it could save one life, it is worth it". Thank you, I will always honor the memory of your daughter and sister and the beautiful kind and caring girl I met.

Thank you Jess for first clearing the way and building the bridge of communication. Reach high Jess, something great is coming your way. Let it happen.

To Robert, for allowing me to re-print your wonderful take on year one. It simply reflected my first year and made me almost jealous.

To Sam, Lizzie, Simon, Nick, Kim and Mark, Emily, and Rob; each of you came to me in so many different ways, all with the same dream: to walk through life unaided by a substance or laden with other comorbid issues. Each of you have achieved that freedom in your own individual wonderful way. Thank you for gracing me with the right to tell your stories.

Mark Quickfall, thank you for stepping up to help me yet again with your vast experience and knowledge, for helping me with the marketing and promotion of this book, but mostly, for once again believing in me.

All of the kind and generous people who donated to the give a little page to help me turn the manuscript into a book. Thank you from the bottom of my heart.

To the New Zealand Embassy in Bangkok, for helping me to get back to my homeland of New Zealand quickly and easily. Khob khun na ka. To Wiremu and Tom from the New Zealand Armed Forces, Tania from the medical team, along with the staff at the Ibis in Rotorua, for making isolation actually fun and humanized with all your gentle, caring, kind, and humorous natures. I sailed through pre-publishing jobs for the book, while you all took care of me. To Brian, you lifted me up, thank you. Im looking forward to your first published book, we both know it's there.

To my wee girl tribe, Antionette and Susan, 'sisters in arms' let the FRWG club continue forever.

My editor Angee Costa who as promised, changed almost nothing, thank you so much for that. Although she did try to turn my swearing down, I turned it back up slightly, as that is just who I am, in the right company, of course. I asked her if she could keep my voice intact, and she did just that, "I'll just fine tune it to make it sing", so what you read is what I wrote in Phuket, Thailand, in '2563' Epochal, Buddhism year, '2020' Covid lockdown year for the rest of the world.

To Gavin's editor, Rainy, thank you for fully 'getting' Gavin's words and understanding his logic and work, and in doing so, it was a joy to see his entire chapter 'shining but intact'.

To Gavin, thank you for being just who you are. The passion and care you put into every single person surpasses anyone I have ever worked with. For your amazing professional input with this book, for making sense of where our troubles can come from, and for showing us the way to acknowledge them and let them go. Thank you for awakening my mind, for explaining me, to me, and for letting me steal your words to try and sound smart. On top of that, for just being a bloody funny, genuine, good bloke.

To all those that matter, you know who you are. Thank you for staying in my life and helping me become comfortable with what makes me, me. We have all grown closer in every way by the ugly and beautiful journey we went through. "Even weeds grow flowers" is representative of the horrors and beauty that trauma, mental health and substance misuse brought to us. Followed by a closer understanding and bonded knowledge, and a deeper appreciation of the love and the good that lies within all of us.

Lastly my boys, Joel, and Jackson, you are the reason my heart beats so strong. You are the warm breeze beneath my wings that lifts me up every beautiful day. You are my arrows that I sent forth from my mother bow, and the direction you each aim for, makes me so proud and full of love for the darling beautiful men you have become. I know with every morsel in my heart, mind, soul and bones, overcoming traumas and surviving alcoholism, to be present as a mother to you both is the greatest gift I could have received from having the strength to look up and reach out for help.

I'd like to honor my late dearest friend Susan with these last words. Neither her nor I were or are religious as such, however, she had a favorite saying. "Girly would you look at the beautiful day the good lord has given us". So yes Susan, I look up and out every day now, and I think, isn't it a beautiful day in a beautiful life, one that I cherish, and one with no bloody excuses.